JARROLD
publishing

D0123832

OXFORD

...MORE THAN A GUIDE

ANNIE BULLEN

CITY-BREAK GUIDES

Acknowledgements
Photography © Jarrold
Publishing by Neil
Jinkerson.
Additional photography
by kind permission of:
The Bate Collection of
Musical Instruments;
Cotswold Wildlife Park;
John Crook; John Curtis;
John Heseltine; Museum
of the History of Science;
Oxford Picture Library;
Pitt Rivers Museum;
Salters Steamers.

The publishers wish to
thank Blue Badge guide
Leatrice Beeson for her
invaluable assistance; also
the many owners of
Oxford businesses for
their kindness in allowing
us to photograph their
premises.

Printed in Singapore.
ISBN 0 7117 2952 2 1/04

Designer:
Simon Borrough
Editor:
Angela Royston
Artwork and walk maps:
Clive Goodyer
City maps:
The Map Studio, Romsey,
Hants. Main map based on
cartography © George
Philip Ltd

Front cover:
**Punts on the River
Cherwell**

Previous page:
Magdalen College

CONTENTS

WELCOME TO OXFORD

'Where's the university?' ask visitors, expecting a neat campus and a few impressive buildings. Oxford University is a tight weaving of 39 colleges and many ancient buildings in and around the city's shops and offices. As you walk, you'll spot great wooden doors, half-open, with enticing views of old

WHAT OTHER PLACE?

When in Oxford don't mention that other great seat of learning, Cambridge. Just do as they do and call it 'The Other Place'.

View of All Souls from
St Mary's Tower

stonework and neatly kept quadrangles.
Grand Palladian entrances are tucked
away behind the shops, little cobbled
streets open out into squares housing
splendid buildings, while narrow
alleyways hide medieval gems. Look up
and you'll see domes and bell-towers,
grandly conceived figures etched against
the skyline and slim spires reaching
towards the clouds.

This is Oxford, city and university intertwined and inseparable, each breathing life into the other. Museums, bookstores, theatre, entertainment of all sorts, excellent pubs, shops, riverside walks and parks and gardens make Oxford a stimulating place to live. Visitors have the added pleasure of exploration and discovery, finding out how the university evolved from a 12th-century 'live-out' teaching establishment for clerics to the grand colleges open to students from many different backgrounds.

Oxford's place as one of our great cities is never in doubt – it excited poet Geoffrey Chaucer in the 14th century and continues to inspire today's writers. There's plenty to excite 21st-century visitors too – use this guide to help you enjoy this most ancient and modern of British cities.

OXFORD-SPEAK

'Proctors' are appointed from college Fellows; they have wide administrative and disciplinary roles. The late Professor Nevill Coghill, a young proctor, said the position made him feel like a combination of Charlie's Aunt and Judas Iscariot.

OXFORD-SPEAK
The academic year is divided into three eight-week terms. But don't call them 'winter', 'spring' and 'summer'. In Oxford the year starts with the Michaelmas term, followed by Hilary and Trinity. At the end of term, undergraduates 'go down' (go home) for the vacation. Being 'sent down' is another matter altogether.

Botanic Garden

HIGHLIGHTS

Oxford offers so much – ancient colleges, magnificent honey-coloured buildings in a variety of styles, wide streets, winding alleyways, interesting pubs and, always, the river – where do you start? Even those who know Oxford well can find something new in this city that has provided the conditions for creativity to flourish over hundreds of years. Here are some of the must-sees and must-dos. Be comforted that once you've visited them all there will be plenty more to keep you occupied.

ROOF WITH A VIEW

It might be an effort, but the best view of the extraordinarily beautiful 'roofscape' of Oxford is gained from a climb to the top of one of the recommended vantage points – all of them buildings of interest in their own right:

Carfax Tower
Queen Street; map C4

Once the medieval church of St Martin stood with its tower at Carfax – the crossroads – in the heart of Oxford. But the church impeded the free flow of traffic and was pulled down in 1896. Now cars have been banished during

Carfax Tower

'O W Z A T !
Oxford University Cricket Club has produced many great sports-
men, including cricketing legends Colin Cowdrey and Imran Khan.

the day (but not other traffic) and only
the tower, with its 'quarter boy' strikers,
stands alone. Climb to the top (99 steps
altogether) for that famous view.
Open: daily, 10.00–17.15 (summer);
10.00–15.30 (winter)
Entry: under £2
Further information: page 39

Sheldonian Theatre
Broad Street; map D3
The sight of the strange, bearded
'guardians' outside the Sheldonian is an
extraordinary one. Inside this wood-
panelled building, used mainly for university ceremonies, concerts and lectures,
you'll notice the lovely painted ceiling full
of lofty allegory. But spare the time to
climb into the cupola for another good
view of the surrounding buildings. You
can buy a map telling you what each
dome, spire, roof and tower is.
Open: Mon–Sat 10.00–16.30 (closes
15.30 in winter)
Entry: under £5
Further information: pages 49–50

Bearded heads outside the
Sheldonian Theatre

P E R F E C T   P R E S C R I P T I O N
Oxford didn't always see eye to eye with the reigning monarch but
Queen Anne, who came to the throne in 1702, had a cordial relation-
ship with the city. Her doctor, John Radcliffe, was even better liked –
his bequests were responsible for the Radcliffe Camera, the
Infirmary and the Observatory that bear his name, and he also paid
for a second quadrangle for University College.

St Michael at the North Gate
Cornmarket Street; map C3

This Saxon tower lays claim to be Oxford's oldest building but it can still be relied on for a wonderful view for those prepared to puff their way to the top.

Open: daily; Apr–Oct: Mon–Sat 10.00–17.00, Sun 12.00–17.00 (closes 16.00 Nov–Mar)
Entry: under £2
Further information: page 49

University Church of St Mary the Virgin
High Street; map D3/D4

This church is still attached to its tower unlike poor St Martin. And the view from the top is just as fine although the climb is a little more strenuous. Beware a trip to the top when the bells are ringing – it can be deafening.

Open: daily; Jul–Aug: 9.00–19.00; Sep–Jun: 9.00–17.00
Entry to tower: under £2
Further information: page 52

Punting on the River Cherwell

BE A PUNTER

You might even be good at propelling these traditional flat-bottomed vessels along the winding stretches of the River Cherwell from Magdalen Bridge (map F4) or Folly Bridge. A 7.5-metre (25-foot) wooden punt will take up to four passengers. Wearing a boater is not obligatory and if you think that wielding a 5-metre (16-foot) pole is not for you, you can always hire a boatman to do the job. Simply turn up at the boating stations at either of the bridges and away you go.

Church of St Mary the Virgin

OXFORD UNION
World-famous for its debating society this student club has its headquarters off Cornmarket. Past presidents include William Gladstone, Robin Day, Ted Heath, Michael Foot, Tariq Ali and Benazir Bhutto.

Sheldonian Theatre

STAR-GAZING

Astronomer Edmund
Halley lived in New
College Lane in the
18th century. It was
from the rooftop obser-
vatory of his house that
he observed the comet
that bears his name.

Trinity College

DO THE COLLEGES

You can't visit Oxford without exploring the colleges. Be warned that opening times can be varied – many shut during examinations and for special functions. Christ Church, Magdalen, Trinity, Brasenose and New College are famous colleges that have much to see and are particularly worth exploring.

Christ Church Cathedral
St Aldates; map D5

Do look in the cathedral at Christ Church, if it is open. Here you'll find the reconstructed shrine of St Frideswide, whose nunnery once stood on the same spot, some wonderful stained glass by Edward Burne-Jones and an extraordinarily beautiful vaulted stone ceiling over the chancel.

There are corners of Harry Potter's Hogwarts School to be glimpsed around the grand dining hall of the college, as much of the filming was done here. Hogwarts dining hall is modelled on that of Christ Church but was 'reconstructed' in the studio – the original was just not big enough for all those young witches and wizards.

Magdalen College
High Street; map F4

Enjoy the gardens at Magdalen and the tiny Chaplain's Quadrangle with David Wynne's beautiful and moving sculpture of Christ with St Mary Magdalen. You can embark on a riverside walk here, watching punters brandishing their poles with varying degrees of expertise.

Further information on these and other colleges open to the public: pages 32–55

Magdalen College

> **TREAT YOURSELF**
> You've seen the reproductions – now seek out the real thing. William Holman Hunt's painting *The Light of the World* hangs in a side chapel at Keble College.

Botanic Garden

GETTING THE BLUES
An Oxford Blue is a sportsperson who has represented the university against Cambridge and has a right to wear the colour – but these days you'll also find Oxford Blue cheese in the Covered Market and Oxford Blue ice cream.

BE A BOOKWORM
Who couldn't enjoy books in Oxford? Start in Broad Street (map C3–D3) where the world-famous Blackwell's dominates with several branches. There's a good Borders in Magdalen Street (map B3), Waterstone's in Broad Street (map C3) and countless specialist and second-hand bookshops all over the city.

PLANT-HUNTERS' PARADISE
High Street; map F4
At the far end of The High (Oxford-speak for the High Street) opposite Magdalen College and Magdalen Bridge is Oxford's Botanic Garden. Plant-lovers will enjoy the range of herbaceous plants and shrubs growing in borders and order beds. If you're not a gardener this is still a lovely place to spend an hour or so, exploring the glasshouses, the lawns and sitting awhile on the riverbank.
Open: daily; Apr–Sep: 9.00–17.00 (glasshouses 10.00–16.30); Oct–Mar: 9.00–17.00 (glasshouses 10.00–16.00); last admission 16.15
Entry: Apr–Sep: under £5; Oct–Mar: by donation
Further information: pages 36–37

LOOKING AT PAINTINGS
Ashmolean Museum
Beaumont Street; map B2
The Ashmolean Museum includes works by Holbein, Gainsborough, Blake, Constable, Manet and Pissaro.
Open: Tue–Sat 10.00–17.00, Sun 14.00–17.00; late opening on Thursday evenings in summer
Entry: free
Further information: page 34

Christ Church Picture Gallery
Oriel Square; map D4
There's a terrific collection, spanning four centuries, of Italian paintings and drawings in the Christ Church Picture Gallery, which can be reached through the college or, independently, by way of Oriel Square. Here you'll see works by Leonardo da Vinci, Michelangelo, Tintoretto and Veronese.
Open: daily; Apr–Sept: Mon–Sat 10.30–17.00; Sun 14.00–17.00; Oct–Mar: Mon–Sat 10.30–13.00 and 14.00–16.30; Sun 14.00–16.30
Entry: £2
Further information: page 40

Modern Art Oxford
Pembroke Street; map C4

If you prefer modern art, visit Modern Art Oxford.

Open: Tue–Sat 10.00–17.00, Sun 12.00–17.00
Entry: free
Further information: page 44

EXPLORING THE PUBS
The Eagle and Child
St Giles; map B2

Oxford's pubs are many and interesting. One of the favourites is The Bird and Baby (properly known as The Eagle and Child). This is where the coyly named 'Inklings', a group of Oxford writers including C.S. Lewis and J.R.R. Tolkien, met every Tuesday in what became known as the 'Rabbit Room' to smoke, drink and discuss lions, witches and hobbits. Just across the way is the equally old and interesting Lamb and Flag.

Ties in The Bear

The Bear
Alfred Street; map C4

One of the tiniest pubs is The Bear, just off The High. Here you'll see that the walls and ceiling in the minute snug bar are covered with snipped-off and neatly labelled ties from all corners of the Earth. Beware a landlord with sharp scissors …

The Turf Tavern
Bath Place; map D3

You'll need a good sense of direction to find this pub, reached only by way of narrow lanes. With a lovely old bar, a huge range of guest beers and a pleasant sitting-out area, it's worth the search.

The White Horse
Broad Street; map D3

This pub is a little easier to find, although no less cosy. The White Horse is squeezed between two branches of Blackwell's Bookshop.

TIME FOR TEA

Afternoon tea can be turned into a special occasion at The Grand Café in The High (map E4). This splendid establishment offers proper tea in traditional

The Grand Café

metal pots with napkins wrapped round the handle to prevent scalding. The cakes are wonderful and you can always go the whole hog with smoked-salmon sandwiches and champagne that will set you back a bit but leave a wonderful taste. The Randolph in Beaumont Street (map B2) offers a similar tea.
Further information: pages 72, 73

Covered Market

VISIT THE MARKET
High Street; map C3–C4
The traditional Covered Market off The High is one of the wonders of Oxford. Fresh fish, meat, fruit and vegetables are the mainstay of this large and bustling market but you'll also find farmhouse cheeses (try the Oxford Blue), beautifully decorated cakes, hats, shoes, knitwear, flowers, books, chocolates – everything that makes life comfortable. In addition there are cafés and sandwich bars whose range varies from full English breakfast through to healthy juice bars. Don't expect this to be a quick visit.
Further information: pages 59–61

DOING LUNCH
North Oxford and the Jericho area are full of good eating places. Try Branca in Walton Street (map A1) for some good, modern Italian cooking or Le Petit Blanc in the same street. Walton Street is where you'll also find Freud, worth visiting for the exotic surroundings alone (it's a deconsecrated church), although the food is good too. Gees in Banbury Road (map B1) serves good food in luxurious surroundings, while the Parsonage Bar and Restaurant, also in Banbury Road, is a good bet too. Lovers of Thai food should try the Chiang Mai Kitchen down the tiny Kemp Hall Passage off The High (map C4).
Further information: pages 72–76

Juice It

Magdalen College

A CITY OF BOOKS

Writer Jan Morris called Oxford a 'city built on books'. There are books about Oxford, books penned by writers living in the city as well as books sold in the dozens of bookshops and read in dozens of libraries in this most literary of places. Oxford's writers reveal different versions of the city, while the city itself retains traces of these writers' lives.

The most recent and fantastical is Philip Pullman's imaginary other-universe Oxford, the starting point for his award-winning fantasy trilogy *His Dark Materials*. Pullman, who lives on the edge of the city, has said that he can't think why a writer should want to live anywhere else. *Lord of the Rings* author J.R.R. Tolkien would have said the same. He and fellow writers C.S. Lewis, Charles Williams and Neville Coghill used to meet in The Eagle and Child pub in St Giles every Tuesday to discuss literature and bring Middle Earth and Narnia to life.

North Oxford, with its rarefied atmosphere, is the setting for Barbara Pym's

The Little Bookshop

gentle observations on intellectual life and love. The late, great Iris Murdoch (first spotted by future husband John Bayley as she pedalled her bicycle down a drizzly Woodstock Road) taught philosophy at St Anne's College before her growing fame as a novelist compelled her to write full time.

College life at its most splendid is celebrated in Evelyn Waugh's *Brideshead Revisited*. 'Oxford, in those days, was still a city of aquatint,' observes Waugh through his Brideshead protagonist, Charles Ryder. Waugh, once an undergraduate at Hertford College (map D3), knew the city well. Waugh's characters gained admittance to the university with ease; the outsider's view is movingly given by Thomas Hardy in *Jude the Obscure*, when his hero can't break the class barrier to be admitted to a thinly disguised 'Christminster'.

Visitors to Christ Church (map C5) will be reminded of the connection to *Alice's Adventures in Wonderland*. Writer Charles Dodgson (Lewis Carroll) was a mathematics tutor at the college from 1855–98. During that time he befriended Alice, the daughter of Dean Henry Liddell, and, using the pseudonym 'Lewis Carroll', Dodgson wove fantasy stories around her life. More recently, writer Colin Dexter has bumped off more than 80 good people of Oxford in his Inspector Morse books, which have translated so well into television. The often morose Morse is, to some, an unlikely policeman, having graduated from the fictitious Lonsdale College.

The Eagle and Child

M Y   W O R D !

Pembroke College remembers with mixed feelings its former student Samuel Johnson, famous lexicographer. Unruly and eccentric, with a reputation for laziness, he rarely left his room during his four terms there in 1728, preferring to talk to friends and drink tea. The college still owns his large teapot.

Blackwell's Bookshop

PLANNING YOUR VISIT

You'll get the feel of Oxford the minute you set foot in it – but it takes a lot longer to see and enjoy all that gives the city its rarified atmosphere. The busy shopping areas are like any others, but walk along The High (High Street) and you'll catch glimpses of another life going on behind the centuries-old wooden doors guarding the quadrangles of ancient colleges.

You'll see eccentrically garbed men and women pedalling ancient bicycles, their minds clearly on higher things. You'll hear phrases you don't quite understand – Oxford-speak, developed over centuries of academic life. But don't feel excluded. Explore, visit the colleges, the museums and the old cobbled streets and you'll soon feel at home. Here are a few suggestions for making the most of your time, whether it is only a few hours or a few days.

Fasta Pasta in the Covered Market

WHAT TO DO IN ONE DAY

Start with breakfast or a cup of coffee in Oxford's ancient Covered Market (see page 71). Go in through any of the four High Street entrances (map C4) or from Market Street (map C3). Take time to wander up and down the aisles, discovering all the varied goods on offer.

Leave by a High Street entrance and walk down to St Aldates to visit Christ Church (map C5) – college and cathedral (see page 39). Legend has it that St Frideswide founded a religious priory on this site in the 8th century. You can see a shrine to her memory in the cathedral's Lady Chapel. Later Thomas Wolsey decided to build a magnificent and ambitious 'Cardinal College' here. Work started but the Cardinal fell out with Henry VIII who took over the project, renamed it Christ Church and rebuilt the priory church of St Frideswide as the city's cathedral.

As you leave Christ Church by the Oriel Square gate, you might like to visit the Picture Gallery (see page 40) in the little cobbled quad by the gate. They have a magnificent collection of (mainly Italian) old master paintings and drawings. Walk back up one of the little lanes leading to The High, cross over and explore the area behind the church of St Mary the Virgin. There are the perfectly round Radcliffe Camera (see page 47) and the Bodleian Library (see page 36). A little further on you'll find Broad Street (it is) with the Sheldonian Theatre (see page 49) standing watch on the corner across the way from Blackwell's famous bookshop.

Time for a drink and lunch at one of Oxford's excellent pubs or restaurants (see pages 72–78) before strolling along The High to Magdalen College (see page 43), where you can enjoy the gardens and riverside walk as much as the ancient buildings.

Afterwards it might be a good idea to cross the road for a peaceful interlude in the Botanic Garden (see page 36) before walking back along The High for a reviving cup of tea at the Queen's Lane Coffee House or the Grand Café.

Magdalen College gardens

WHAT TO DO IN THE NEXT TWO OR THREE DAYS

If you managed to squeeze all the suggestions above into one day, you'll have some idea of the grand scale of the university, its colleges and buildings. Here are some 'pick-and-mix' suggestions for the rest of your visit:

Go to Jericho

North Oxford, they say, is one of the last refuges of the true English eccentric. These days that part of the city is the place to be and there's no doubt that Jericho, stretching to the north and west of Little Clarendon Street (map B1) is an increasingly popular and trendy area as you can see by the restaurants, cafés, shops and the art-house cinema here. The area is named after Jericho Gardens, which once stood here.

It's just a five-minute walk from the city centre up to Jericho's Little Clarendon Street and Walton Street (map A1), where you'll find interesting shops and some very good pubs and restaurants. Here too are the rather splendid classical buildings of the Oxford University Press (OUP), unfortunately not open to the public. Turn down one of the narrow streets by the OUP to come upon the Oxford Canal with its gatherings of picturesque boats. You'll also find St Barnabas Church with its landmark Italianate tower, built in 1869 by the then head of the OUP for the local people.

Hit the heights

Get some idea of Oxford's magnificent skyline by climbing to the top of one of the four main vantage points in the city centre: the Sheldonian cupola, St Mary's Tower, Carfax Tower or the tower of St Michael at the North Gate (see pages 8–10). Each of the places will tell you about what you can see.

Enjoy the history

The Ashmolean Museum (see page 34) is a treasure-house of archaeological artefacts. It also holds an internationally important art collection. Not too far away is the fascinating double act of the University Museum of Natural History (complete with dinosaurs) and the Pitt Rivers Museum, next to each other in Parks Road (see pages 52 and 46).

University Museum of Natural History

Radcliffe Camera

Lamb and Flag Passage

Oxford on foot

For an interesting insight into the history of Oxford, join one of the daily guided walks round the city. If that sounds like hard work, you could try a sightseeing tour by bus (see page 83). There are some suggestions for 'do-it-yourself' walks on pages 26–31.

Time travel

The Oxford Story (see page 46) is an excellent and entertaining introduction to Oxford from earliest times to the present day. Sit down at a 'desk' to learn all about it – and be whisked away down the corridors of time.

A breath of fresh air

Visit the Covered Market and put together the ingredients for a picnic to enjoy in one of the many parks and green spaces in the city (see pages 56–57). Or hire a bike (see page 94) and enjoy a ride along the canal towpath. The braver might like to try a spot of punting but, if that seems too hands-on, there's the option of a steamer trip up the river (see page 83).

Explore the colleges

We've suggested a couple of college visits on the first day but there are plenty more to see. They're open mostly in the afternoon – see pages 32–55 for details. Please remember that many colleges close when exams are in progress.

Brasenose College

CLARENDON BUILDING

The elegant Clarendon Building in The Broad was designed by Hawksmoor as a new home for the Oxford University Press, which uses the Clarendon Press imprint to this day. OUP outgrew the building and moved to Walton Street, while the Clarendon Building with its fine wrought-iron gates became office space for the university.

Alpha Bar in the
Covered Market

STREET-WISE
If you want to sound
like a local don't say
High Street or Broad
Street. Just refer airily
to 'The High', 'The
Broad', 'The Turl',
and so forth.

WALKS

There are excellent daily guided walks starting from the Tourist Information Centre in Broad Street (see page 94), and this section gives two walks linked to literary themes and another which will guide you around some of the best shopping streets. Each walk will take about an hour – or more, if you linger along the way.

Dead Man's Walk

REVISIT BRIDESHEAD WALK

This walk will take you to some of the places and buildings mentioned in Evelyn Waugh's classic novel, *Brideshead Revisited*. The story is told by lonely student Charles Ryder, who is invited to lunch at Christ Church by the utterly charming and beautiful Sebastian Flyte. The walk starts and ends in St Aldates at Christ Church where Sebastian had his rooms high in the Venetian-style Meadow Building. You can't go in but you'll pass through the building as you enter the college. Christ Church was where the outrageously camp aesthete Anthony Blanche also lived. Anthony, telling Charles about the night he was thrown into the fountain, speaks of watching the light fade on the walls of Peckwater Quad. The quad stands on the site of a medieval inn, run by the Peckwater family. Anthony's ducking took place right in the centre of

Christ Church's Tom Quad where a statue of Mercury enlivens the fishpond.

After that first lunch in Meadow Building Charles and Sebastian made their way to the Botanic Garden 'to see the ivy'. They would have walked out of the main entrance towards the meadow and along the footpaths to the so-called 'Dead Man's

Walk' under the walls of Merton College and up Rose Lane to the Garden. Follow them and enjoy the plants and the views over the river before reaching the High Street. Turn left along The High until you see Queen's Lane on the right. Cross over and follow this road into New College Lane, passing by Hertford College where Brideshead author Evelyn Waugh was a student.

Continue round to Broad Street where Charles, devastated by Anthony's condemnation of Sebastian and his family, took a lonely breakfast in a teashop opposite Balliol.

Walk down Cornmarket Street past the 'venerable arch' of the Golden Cross on the left, through which Charles saw a group of his friends. The arch is now an entrance to the covered market. At Carfax Tower Charles met the Mayor and corporation, processing to church at St Mary's. Like Charles, cross over to St Aldates and return to Christ Church.

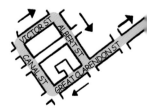

INSPECTOR MORSE WALK

This walk links some of the places featured in Colin Dexter's Inspector Morse books and shown in the television series. It is not exactly a pub crawl, but Detective Chief Inspector Morse did occasionally enjoy a pint or two.

Start, appropriately, at The Randolph Hotel's Morse Bar in Beaumont Street. This was the setting for *The Jewel That Was Ours* (television's *The Wolvercote Tongue*), where a group of Americans stay on their 'historic England' tour. Move on to the Ashmolean Museum where you can see the Alfred Jewel, an Anglo-Saxon gem that was the inspiration for 'The Wolvercote Tongue', which went missing just after its owner died in mysterious circumstances.

Now it's a small trek by way of Walton Street, Great Clarendon Street and Canal Street over to Victor Street in Jericho, where The Old Bookbinders Ale House provided refreshment to help the detective's thought processes in *The Dead of Jericho*. In the novel the pub is called 'The Printer's Devil'.

Retrace your steps to Walton Street and follow Little Clarendon Street to St Giles. Here you'll find the much-visited Eagle and Child public house where Morse and Lewis were known to take the weight off their feet. Cross the road, and continue down Lamb and Flag Passage to Museum Road and across Parks Road to the Pitt Rivers Museum, which you access through the Natural History Museum. This was where the knife-wielding Ted Brooks stole his murder weapon in *The Daughters of Cain*.

Now it's back down Parks Road and Holywell Street to Bath Place in the heart of the city to the tucked-away Turf Tavern. This pub, with its excellent beer, also features in *The Daughters of Cain*. It's no more than a few steps from the Turf to the Sheldonian Theatre in Broad Street, where opera diva Gladys Probert was assassinated in *The Twilight of the Gods* as she walked in procession across the square.

Morse Bar at The Randolph Hotel

The Old Bookbinders Ale House

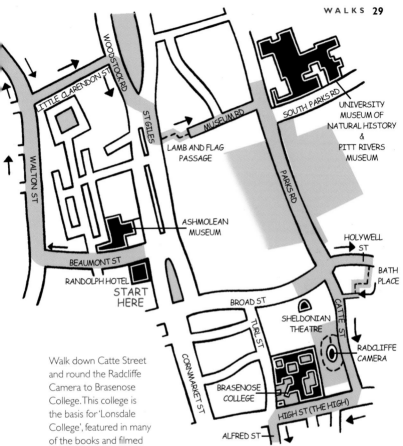

WOODSTOCK RD

LITTLE CLARENDON ST

ST GILES

MUSEUM RD

SOUTH PARKS RD

UNIVERSITY
MUSEUM OF
NATURAL HISTORY
&
PITT RIVERS
MUSEUM

LAMB AND FLAG
PASSAGE

PARKS RD

WALTON ST

ASHMOLEAN
MUSEUM

HOLYWELL
ST

BEAUMONT ST

BATH
PLACE

RANDOLPH HOTEL

**START
HERE**

BROAD ST

SHELDONIAN
THEATRE

CATTE ST

TURL ST

RADCLIFFE
CAMERA

CORNMARKET ST

BRASENOSE
COLLEGE

HIGH ST (THE HIGH)

ALFRED ST

Walk down Catte Street
and round the Radcliffe
Camera to Brasenose
College. This college is
the basis for 'Lonsdale
College', featured in many
of the books and filmed
for television. Brasenose
is open to visitors most
afternoons (see page 37).
Walk down to The High,
turn right and then cross
the road to Alfred Street,
where you'll find just one
more pub – The Bear,
where Morse carried out
his investigations in *Death
is Now My Neighbour*.

T R E A D   C A R E F U L L Y
The path that runs from Christ Church
Meadow, below the wall of Merton College,
to the Botanic Garden is known as 'Dead
Man's Walk'. This is said to have dated from
the 13th century when a Jewish cemetery
occupied the site where the Botanic Garden
now stands.

STOPPING TO SHOP WALK

Oxford has some excellent small shops but they are scattered around the city. Here is a suggested route that takes you to many of the best shopping streets – use it along with the shopping guide on pages 58–69. There are plenty of refreshment stops along the way.

Start at the Covered Market off The High – there's plenty of variety here and it's good for coffee too. Leave by way of Golden Cross Walk and turn right into Cornmarket Street, where you'll find many High-Street names. Carry on

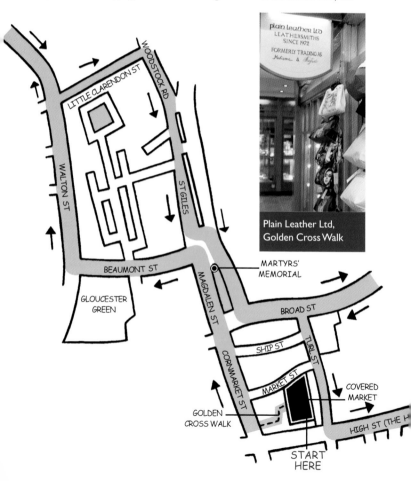

Plain Leather Ltd, Golden Cross Walk

WOODSTOCK RD

LITTLE CLARENDON ST

ST GILES

WALTON ST

BEAUMONT ST

GLOUCESTER GREEN

MAGDALEN ST

MARTYRS' MEMORIAL

BROAD ST

SHIP ST

TURL ST

CORNMARKET ST

MARKET ST

COVERED MARKET

GOLDEN CROSS WALK

HIGH ST (THE H

START HERE

up Magdalen Street and turn left along Beaumont Street. To your left you'll find Gloucester Green with its shops and regular Wednesday markets. The popular Farmers' Market is held here on the first Thursday of each month.

Turn right into Walton Street, past the residential houses, until you come to Little Clarendon Street on your right. There are very good fashion and household shops down here. Either carry on up Walton Street to explore more shops, restaurants and pubs or turn immediately into Little Clarendon Street back towards St Giles. Walk down towards the Martyrs' Memorial, perhaps stopping off at

Farmers' Market

TREAT YOURSELF
Blow the diet and enjoy a real old-fashioned tea with exquisite cakes, sandwiches and maybe a glass of champagne. The Grand Café (in The High), The Randolph (in Beaumont Street) and Maison Blanc (in Woodstock Road) are all recommended.

The Randolph for a little refreshment. Keep to the left-hand side of the wide street until you see Broad Street on your left. Here you'll find bookshops galore and other shops as well. When you've explored Broad Street, turn down picturesque Turl Street towards The High. Now you've got the whole of Oxford's grandest street to explore before collapsing in the nearest café or pub.

Golden Cross Walk

Sheldonian Theatre

SIGHTSEEING

The ancient and beautiful college buildings are the lure for most visitors to this elegant city. But you'll be pleasantly surprised at the other attractions, many of them free or charging a nominal sum. Most are open all year round but closed on Christmas Day and Boxing Day and some over the Easter weekend.

Most colleges are mainly open to the public in the afternoon. The opening times given in this section are a guide only, depending on examinations, holidays and functions, so check first if you are making a special journey. Disabled access is limited because of the nature of the buildings – please ring first to check on wheelchair access. You'll notice that you are asked to visit quietly, remembering that students are living and working there; you are also asked to visit only those areas open to the public.

All Souls College
High Street; map D3
The 'twin towers' of All Souls, the work of Hawksmoor, are in the college's North (or Great) Quad, but their impressive height allows glimpses of them as you walk round the city. Hawksmoor also designed the newly renovated Codrington Library on the far side of the quad. The sundial was designed by Christopher Wren. You will find it on the wall of the Codlington Library. All Souls is unique in that there are no undergraduates – all fellows are eminent graduates whose work is mainly academic research.
Open: Mon–Fri 14.00–16.00
Entry: free (please ring in advance if you are a group of more than six)
Tel: 01865 279379
Website: www.all-souls.ox.ac.uk

All Souls College

Ashmolean Museum

Ashmolean Museum
Beaumont Street; map B2

The basis of the original collection in this, one of the first museums in Britain, were the rarities scooped up by plant-hunters, father and son John Tradescant in the 17th century. The ownership of the Tradescant collection of fauna (dead and preserved), coins, shells, weapons and much more besides was disputed for years by Mrs Tradescant, who was reluctant to see it leave the family home in Lambeth, and Elias Ashmole, friend of the younger plant-hunter. Eventually Ashmole, a great collector, prevailed and the collection was housed in Broad Street, Oxford, for the public to marvel at. But both the Ashmolean Museum and the Tradescant Collection moved house – the former to a new neo-classical building in Beaumont Street and the latter to the Pitt Rivers Museum and the University Museum of Natural History (see pages 46 and 52).

Now the Ashmolean houses a terrific collection of archaeological artefacts and great paintings, including works by Titian, Holbein, Rembrandt, Gainsborough, Blake, Constable, Manet, Pissaro and Degas. There's also a good programme of events – and plenty for children to do and see.

DON'T MISS
The Alfred Jewel: a large Anglo-Saxon gem of gold and rock crystal with an enamel plaque showing a figure variously thought to be Christ, St Cuthbert, St Neot or King Alfred himself. A gold inscription round the edge of the jewel reads 'Alfred ordered my making'.
The Scorpion King: a huge mace head from 3100 BC showing an Egyptian ruler with a carved scorpion.
The Weld-Blundell Prism: a clay 'prism' inscribed in Sumerian with lists of rulers from 3200–1800 BC. It is named after the man who gave it to the museum.
Open: Tue–Sat 10.00–17.00, Sun 14.00–17.00; late opening on summer Thursday evenings
Entry: free
Tel: 01865 278000
Website: www.ashmol.ox.ac.uk
Disabled access: reasonable – they like you to check first so that they can offer all possible help
Other facilities: shop and café

Balliol College
Broad Street; map C3

Founded as an act of penance in 1263 by John Balliol, this college was originally reserved for poor scholars. But it came into its own in Victorian times when successive masters steered it in the direction of academic excellence and achieving 'effortless superiority'. Poets and writers, including Gerard Manley Hopkins, Matthew Arnold, Algernon Charles Swinburne, Aldous Huxley, Graham Green, Anthony Powell and Nevil Shute, were all Balliol men – as were politicians Harold Macmillan, Edward Heath, Denis Healey and Roy Jenkins.

Open: daily 14.00–17.00
Entry: £1
Tel: 01865 277777
Website:
www.balliol.ox.ac.uk

Harpsichord
at the Bate
Collection

Bate Collection of Musical Instruments
Faculty of Music,
St Aldates; map C5

Have you ever seen a seven-key serpent? Do you know what it is? This wonderful, wiggly woodwind instrument, made by Thomas Key in 1810, is one of many beautifully preserved and well-looked-after musical treasures in the Bate Collection, which belongs to the Faculty of Music. Perhaps the most impressive 'instrument' you'll see here is the Javanese Gamelan – not one instrument at all but an assembly of gongs and metal-lophones. This Gamelan is called 'Kyai Madu Laras' which means 'venerable sweet harmony'. Like many of the pieces in the collection, it is still played regularly.

Open: Mon–Fri 14.00–17.00, Sat (term time only) 10.00–12.00
Entry: free
Tel: 01865 276139
Website: www. music.ox.ac.uk
Disabled access: limited
Other facilities: shop

Blackwell's bookshop
Broad Street; map C3

It is hard to believe that the original shop, opened by Benjamin Henry Blackwell in 1879, was at first so small that only three customers could squeeze inside. Now it is one of the largest book-shops in the world with a basement, the Norrington Room, that extends under Trinity College and is said to have 5 km (3 miles) of shelving.

Balliol College

Vaulted stone ceiling in Divinity School

Statue of William Herbert, Old Schools Quadrangle

Bodleian Library
Broad Street; map D3

Don't expect just one building to house the immense collection of the most famous library in the world. The Bodleian is not only the main research library for the university but also holds a copy of every book published and is used by scholars around the world. The buildings include Duke Humfrey's Library above the Divinity School, the Old Schools Quadrangle, the Radcliffe Camera and the Clarendon Building. Other specialist sections are scattered around the city. Although you can't visit many parts of the Bodleian you can have a look round the Divinity School (note the wonderful ceiling) and the Exhibition Room, or you can join a guided tour and see a little more.
Open: Mon–Fri 9.00–17.00; Sat 9.30–12.30; guided tours of the Divinity School, Convocation House and Duke Humfrey's Library: Mon–Fri 10.30, 11.30, 14.00 and 15.00; Sat 10.30 and 11.30
Entry: free for individual visits; under £5 for the tour
Tel: 01865 277224
Disabled access: very limited
Other facilities: shop

Botanic Garden
High Street; map F4

Plantaholics visit this lovely botanic garden (the oldest in Britain) to inspect the national collection of euphorbia, one of two held in this country, and the other plant collections neatly displayed in order beds. Others enjoy the peace of a beautiful garden, bounded by old walls and by the River Cherwell. You are welcome to picnic in the garden.

Botanic Garden

Entry: Apr–Sep: under £5; Oct–Mar: by donation
Tel: 01865 286690
Website: www. botanic-garden.ox.ac.uk
Disabled access: full

Brasenose College
Radcliffe Square; map D3
You'll find the original 'brazen-nose', after which the college is named, in the dining hall. This is a bronze (brazen) sanctuary door-knocker in the shape of the head of an heraldic animal. When you're in the hall look closely at the oriel window by the high table to see stained-glass representations of the knocker. If the weather's fine the tiny quad known as the 'deer park' is a pleasant place to sit. Brasenose College is the 'Lonsdale College' of Colin Dexter's 'Inspector Morse' books and television adaptations.

Botanists will tell you that there is more biodiversity in this comparatively small garden than in a whole tropical rainforest. The prime purpose of a botanic garden is to grow plants for reference, research, conservation and academic reasons. Here they are beautifully laid out and in addition there are water and rock gardens, autumn borders and an innovative border full of 'black' plants with dark leaves and flowers. Whatever you do, don't mention the ragwort. Oxford ragwort (*Senecio squalidus*), collected from the slopes of Mount Etna, 'escaped' from this garden at the end of the 18th century and wafted across the city, taking root as it went. Now it can be found over almost all of England. Part of the plant collection may be seen at the Harcourt Arboretum, 10 km (6 miles) south of Oxford (see page 41).
Open: daily; Apr–Sep: 9.00–17.00 (glasshouses 10.00–16.30); Oct–Mar: 9.00–17.00 (glasshouses 10.00–16.00); last admission 16.15

Open: daily 10.00–11.30 (groups only), 14.00–16.30 for individual visits
Entry: under £5 (group charge varies – ring for details)
Tel: 01865 277830
Website: www.bnc.ox.ac.uk

Knocker in Brasenose College

Carfax Tower
Queen Street; map C4

You'll notice the smartly painted blue and gold 'quarter boys' or 'quarter jacks' in Roman military uniform on the outside of this tower, once the belfry of St Martin's Church. They are replicas of the originals but they still strike the time every 15 minutes. The climb up the 99 steps to the top of the 14th-century tower is well worth the view of the Oxford skyline.

Open: daily; summer: 10.00–17.15; winter: 10.00–15.30
Entry: under £2
Tel: 01865 792653/726871
Website: www.oxford.gov.uk
Disabled access: none

Christ Church
St Aldates; map C5

This is the grandest of all the Oxford colleges and its chapel is the only one in the world to serve as a cathedral. It was destined to be called 'Cardinal College' after its first founder, Cardinal Wolsey, who conceived a college to outdo all others. But in 1529, his great vision only half completed, the Cardinal fell out with King Henry VIII and the monarch took over the building of Christ Church – both the college and the cathedral. When you visit you'll see Christopher Wren's 'Tom Tower' housing the great bell which is tolled 101 times every night at precisely 21.05.

The college, usually called 'The House', was where Sebastian Flyte lived during his Oxford days in Evelyn Waugh's novel *Brideshead Revisited*, while parts of it were the setting or the inspiration for

Tom Tower, Christ Church

Cathedral, Christ Church

sections of Hogwarts School of Witchcraft and Wizardry in the Harry Potter films. Christ Church was where Charles Dodgson – who wrote under the name of Lewis Carroll – lived for 47 years, first as an undergraduate and then as a maths don. He befriended Alice, the daughter of the dean, weaving wondrous stories around their Oxford lives, eventually creating one of our best-loved children's books, *Alice's Adventures in Wonderland.*

Open: daily, Mon–Sat 9.00–17.30, Sun 12.00–17.30
Entry: under £5
Tel: 01865 286573
Website: www.chch.ox.ac.uk
Other facilities: gift shop

Christ Church Picture Gallery
Oriel Square; map D4

This gallery, which can be visited independently of the college, has a wonderful collection of Italian paintings spanning four centuries, including works by Veronese, Tintoretto and Fillipino Lippi. There are drawings too – Leonardo, Michelangelo and Dürer are among the artists. You'll also find works by Raphael and Rubens. The displays change regularly, as there is not room for all the works to be shown together.

Open: daily; Apr–Sept: Mon–Sat 10.30–17.00, Sun 14.00–17.00; Oct–Mar: Mon–Sat 10.30–13.00 and 14.00–16.30, Sun 14.00–16.30
Entry: £2
Tel: 01865 276172
Website: www.chch.ox.ac.uk/gallery
Disabled access: none

Corpus Christi College
Merton Street; map D4

This is a small college with a pretty front quad. You'll notice the unusual sundial showing a pelican pecking its breast to feed its young with blood (this represents Corpus Christi – the Body of Christ). The 16th-century sculptor was Charles Turnbull, but the original pelican became so badly eroded that she has been replaced by a copy carved by Oxford sculptor Michael Black.

Open: daily 13.30–16.30
Entry: free
Tel: 01865 276700
Website: www.ccc.ox.ac.uk

Corpus Christi sundial

Covered Market
High Street; map C4 or Market Street; map C3

There's been a market here since 1772 when it became imperative to clear the streets which were cluttered with hundreds of insanitary stalls. In those days only meat was sold here and there were at least 40 butchers' shops in the market. Now you'll still find meat but also fish, fresh produce of all sorts, several cafés and sandwich shops, bookshops, chocolate, cakes, clothing, delicatessens and florists.

Open: daily 8.30–17.30
Website: www. oxfordcity.co.uk

Exeter College
Turl Street; map C3

Inspector Morse fans know that the lavishly decorated college chapel, with its Burne-Jones and William Morris tapestry, is where their favourite Chief Inspector listens to his last piece of music (*In Paradisum*) before collapsing on the lawn outside, dying later in the John Radcliffe hospital. Although Exeter is one of Oxford's oldest colleges (founded in 1314 by the then Bishop of Exeter), most of its building including the chapel (1860) is much later and constructed in the Gothic style.

Open: daily 14.00–17.00
Entry: free
Tel: 01865 279600
Website: www.exeter.ox.ac.uk

Exeter College Chapel

Harcourt Arboretum
Nuneham Courtney, 10 km (6 miles) south of Oxford on the A4074

This is the 32-hectare (80-acre) 'out of town' sister of the Botanic Garden (see page 36). There's a 4-hectare (10-acre) woodland garden and a huge 15-hectare (37-acre) meadow ablaze with flowers in the summer.

Open: May–Oct: daily 10.00–17.00; Nov–April: Mon–Fri 10.00–16.30
Entry: free but there is a £2 car parking charge
Tel: 01865 343501
Website: www. botanic-garden.ox.ac.uk
Disabled access: full

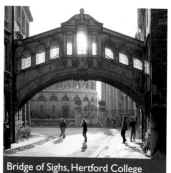

Bridge of Sighs, Hertford College

Hertford College
Catte Street; map D3

The famous 'Bridge of Sighs', arching gracefully over New College Lane, unites two quads and the buildings of Hertford College. Writer Evelyn Waugh used his experiences as an undergraduate here in the 1920s as the material for his best-loved work *Brideshead Revisited*.

Open: daily 10.00–12.00, 14.00–dusk
Entry: free
Tel: 01865 279400
Website: www.hertford.ox.ac.uk

Jesus College
Turl Street; map C3

When Hugh Price set up Jesus College in 1571 he was treasurer of St David's Cathedral, Pembroke, and anxious that this new college should serve Welsh students. Even today a good proportion of Jesus undergraduates come from Wales. T.E. Lawrence (Lawrence of Arabia) and former Prime Minister Harold Wilson were both students here. Turl Street is named for the turnstile or 'twirl' gate that once stood at its Broad Street end.

Open: daily 14.00–16.30
Entry: free
Tel: 01865 279700
Website: www.jesus.ac.ox.uk

Keble College
Parks Road; map C1

The high-minded and entirely praise-worthy motive of providing opportunities at Oxford for poorer students prompted the leaders of the Oxford Movement to ask the public to subscribe to a new college. That was in 1866, just after the death of the founder of the Movement, John Keble. Two years later work began on the interesting design that was likened to a 'dinosaur in a Fair Isle sweater'. But even if critics found the brightly patterned brick alarming, the building itself is well proportioned and the chapel, full of glowing mosaics, houses Holman Hunt's painting *The Light of the World*.

Open: daily 14.00–17.00
Entry: free
Tel: 01865 272727
Website: www.keble.ox.ac.uk

Lincoln College
Turl Street; map C3

Lincoln College library

If you ask the porter as you enter the college, you will probably be able to see the room occupied by John Wesley, founder of Methodism. A graduate of Christ Church, Wesley became a fellow at Lincoln in 1726. Much of the building at Lincoln is original – and the college library is housed in All Saints Church next door. Some of the students have their rooms in the nearby Mitre, once a famous coaching inn and now part of a restaurant chain.

Open: daily; Mon–Sat 14.00–17.00, Sun 11.00–17.00
Entry: free
Tel: 01865 279800
Website: www.linc.ox.ac.uk

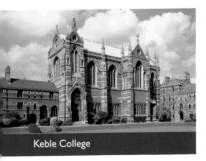

Keble College

Magdalen College
High Street; map F4

Most of the grotesque carved heads, figures and animals that you'll see on postcards from Oxford embellish the walls of Magdalen (always say 'maudlin'), which is one of the richest colleges in the city. Many are caricatures of people who once lived and worked in the college. Magdalen has lovely cloisters and beautiful grounds; if you visit in late April, you'll see the riverside meadow is a haze

of pink and white snakeshead fritillaries. The college's beautiful bell tower, hung with 10 bells, is the setting for a dawn 'concert' every May Day, when the college choir climbs to the roof of the tower and sings to the revellers below, who respond by enjoying champagne breakfasts on the banks of the River Cherwell.

Magdalen College gardens

Martyrs' Memorial

Open: daily; Apr–Jun 13.00–18.00; Jul–Sep 12.00–18.00; Oct–Mar 13.00–dusk
Entry: under £5
Tel: 01865 276000
Website: www.magd.ox.ac.uk

Martyrs' Memorial
St Giles; map C2

It wasn't until nearly 300 years after their deaths that this dignified memorial was built in honour of Archbishop Thomas Cranmer and Bishops Nicholas Ridley and Hugh Latimer, three churchmen who were burned at the stake for upholding the Protestant faith in Queen Mary's Roman Catholic England. Sir George Gilbert Scott designed the monument in 1841, and the statues of the three men were carved by Henry Weekes. Cranmer faces north, holding his Bible, Ridley looks towards the east, while Latimer has his arms crossed and head bowed westwards.

Merton College
Merton Street; map D4–D5

As you go through the gate, look up at the carving (1420) of the lamb, unicorn and lion with John the Baptist and a kneeling bishop, thought to be the college's founder Walter de Merton. This is one of the oldest colleges in Oxford and its Mob Quad is the oldest in the city. Crane your neck again at the far corner of the Front Quadrangle to see the carvings of the signs of the zodiac on

Merton College

Carved stone frieze, Merton College

the vaulted ceiling of the Fitzjames
Gateway. The chapel is one of the finest
in Oxford.
Open: daily; Mon–Fri 14.00–16.00,
Sat–Sun 10.00–16.00
Entry: free for grounds; Old Library
tours may be available for around £1
Tel: 01865 276310
Website: www.merton.ox.ac.uk

Modern Art Oxford
Pembroke Street; map C4
This is the modernized successor to the
acclaimed Museum of Modern Art
(MOMA) and displays work by Tracey
Emmins, David Gorblatt, Yoko Ono and
other notable artists. The new-look
galleries are every bit as exciting as
those that went before them and, in
some ways, they make a refreshing
change from the traditional beauty of
the Oxford street-scene.
Open: Tue–Sat 10.00–17.00, Sun
12.00–17.00
Entry: free
Tel: 01865 722733
Website: www.
modernartoxford.org.uk
Disabled access: full
Other facilities: café

Museum of the History of Science
Broad Street; map C3
More than 10,000 objects used by scientists over the centuries, including
Einstein's blackboard, are displayed here.
This elegant building with its fine oak
staircase was the first Ashmolean
Museum, opened in 1688. Now it
houses astrolabes, early mathematical
instruments, sundials of all sorts, optical
instruments such as telescopes, micro-
scopes and cameras, and a lot more. It is
used by historians as well as by the
general public.
Open: Tue–Sat 12.00–16.00, Sun
14.00–17.00
Entry: free:
Tel: 01865 277280
Website: www.mhs.ox.ac.uk
Disabled access: limited

Medieval astrolabe, Museum of the
History of Science

Museum of Oxford
St Aldates; map C4
As you would expect, this museum tells
the story of the city and the university.
A walk through a series of rooms gives

Museum of Oxford

New College

you a good idea of domestic life. You can also see archaeological treasures, fine paintings and furniture, a college barge and the town's first charter of 1192.

Open: Tue–Fri 10.00–16.00, Sat 10.00–17.00, Sun 12.00–16.00
Entry: under £5
Tel: 01865 252761
Website: www.oxford.gov.uk
Disabled access: none
Other facilities: gift shop

New College
New College Lane; map D3
'New' is a comparative term – this college was founded in 1379 by William of Wykeham when its students all came from his other foundation, Winchester College. The gardens and cloisters are peaceful and timeless while the chapel is particularly fine. Look below its west window for Jacob Epstein's sculpture, *Lazarus* (1951).

Open: daily; Easter–Oct: 11.00–17.00 (New College Lane gates); Oct–Easter: 14.00–16.00 (Holywell Street gates)
Entry: Easter–Oct around £2, Oct–Easter free
Tel: 01865 279555
Website: www.new.ox.ac

Oriel College
Oriel Square; map D4
The real name of this, one of the earliest colleges to be founded, is 'The House of the Blessed Mary the Virgin in Oxford'. Some say the name 'Oriel' comes from an ancient house, L'Oriole, once on the site, others from the oriel windows adorning the building. You'll see testimony to Oxford's fierce loyalty to the Royalists during the Civil War in the carved words *Regnante Carolo* ('When Charles reigns') carved in the ornate parapet above the steps of the grand porch.

Open: daily 14.00–17.00
Entry: free
Tel: 01865 276555
Website: www.oriel.ox.ac.uk

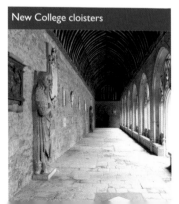

New College cloisters

Oriel College

The Oxford Story
6 Broad Street; map C3

Hop aboard a mechanical desk to
explore 800 years of university history
during a 45-minute 'dark' ride through
the sights, sounds – and smells – of this
city's fascinating past. You'll encounter not
only the riots of the 14th century, but
also Alice in Wonderland, the ups and
downs of college life and some of the
amazing discoveries made in Oxford.
Narration is by an Oxford 'old boy' –
Magnus Magnusson (Jesus College
1948–51) and you'll hear about the writers, scientists and eccentrics who are all
part of the city's bright history. At the
end of the ride you can use the touch
screen of the Innovate Exhibition which
gives an insight into university life today.

Open: daily; Jan–Jun: Mon–Sat
10.00–16.30, Sun 11.00–16.30;
July–Aug: 9.30–17.00; Sept–Dec:
Mon–Sat 10.00–16.30, Sun:
11.00–16.30. Closed Christmas Day
Entry: under £10
Tel: 01865 728822
Website: www.oxfordstory.co.uk
Disabled access: full, but disabled
visitors should be accompanied by
two people; best to phone ahead

Pitt Rivers Museum
Parks Road; map C1

This museum is reached through the
University Museum of Natural History
(see page 52). You'll find it hard to know
where to start in this gloriously cluttered
collection of objects from around the
world. Glass cases stuffed full of meticu-
lously labelled exhibits line the walls and
fill the large rooms. But there is order
and logic here. The objects are shown
according to type so that the visitor can
see the development of ideas world-
wide. You'll find musical instruments,
weapons, masks, textiles, currency,

jewellery, tools, fetishes and much, much more, including 150 objects collected during Captain James Cook's voyage to the South Pacific. It's probably a good idea to explore a section at a time, made possible by free entry to this wonderful collection. The basis of the ethnographic display was the gift of Lieutenant General Augustus Henry Lane Fox Pitt Rivers of around 18,000 objects. That was in 1884. Today the museum shows around half a million pieces. If you really don't know where to start when you walk in, hire an audio guide (narrated by David Attenborough and Brian Rix). The museum is a major teaching resource for the university.

Pitt Rivers Museum

Open: daily; Mon–Sat 12.00–16.30, Sun 14.00–16.30. Closed 24–26 Dec
Entry: free
Tel: 01865 270927
Website: www.prm.ox.ac.uk
Disabled access: very limited; if you phone ahead they will do their best to help
Other facilities: shop

Radcliffe Camera

Radcliffe Camera
Radcliffe Square, off Catte Street; map D3
You can't go inside this most notable of Oxford buildings as it is now the principal reading room of the nearby Bodleian Library. However you can marvel at the circular domed building built between 1737 and 1749 to house the great collection of books belonging to Dr John Radcliffe, Queen Anne's medical adviser. The idea of a rotunda came from architect Nicholas Hawksmoor, but he died before work started so James Gibbs made the final design. The doctor's book collection is now stored in the Radcliffe Science Library.

CONFUSED?
When is a student not a student? At Christ Church, where the undergraduates (and postgraduates) are called 'junior members', while the tutors are given the title 'student'.

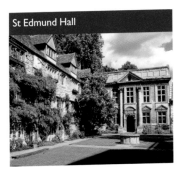

St Edmund Hall

St Edmund Hall

Queen's Lane, map E3

Teddy Hall, as the college is fondly called, is the only one of the dozens of medieval academic halls to survive as a college. Its garden-like front quad is an Oxford favourite. You can see some fine stained glass by Edward Burne-Jones and William Morris in the chapel. The tiny church of St Peter-in-the-East now houses the library.

Open: daily 14.00–17.00
Entry: free
Tel: 01865 279000
Website: www.seh.ox.ac.uk

St John's College

St Giles; map C2

St John's is one of the richest of Oxford's colleges, with grand gardens and buildings. The dignified and ornate Canterbury Quad was paid for by Archbishop of Canterbury William Laud, president of the college from 1611–21.

Open: daily 13.00–17.00 (or dusk if earlier)
Entry: free
Tel: 01865 277300
Website: www.sjc.ox.ac.uk

Canterbury Quad, St John's College

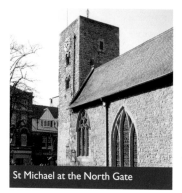

St Michael at the North Gate

St Michael at the North Gate
Cornmarket Street; map C3

The Saxon tower of St Michael is Oxford's oldest building and one of the best viewpoints over the city. Designer William Morris was married here and John Wesley preached in the church.

Open: daily; Apr–Oct: Mon–Sat 10.00–17.00, Sun 12.00–17.00 (closes 16.00 Nov–Mar)
Entry to tower: under £2
Tel: 01865 240940
Website: www.achurchnearyou.com
Disabled access: limited
Other facilities: gift shop and café

OXFORD MOVEMENT
A desire to revive the spirit of early Christianity inspired several eminent Fellows of Oriel to form the Oxford Movement. John Keble, John Newman (who later became a Roman Catholic and a Cardinal) and Thomas Arnold were among the prime movers.

Sheldonian Theatre
Broad Street; map D3

It's a surprise as you turn into Broad Street from Holywell Street to be confronted by an extraordinary semi-circle of 13 carved stone heads, bearded and serene, gazing across to Blackwell's bookshop. These are sculptor Michael Black's modern copies based on the originals by Christopher Wren, who as a young architect was commissioned to design the building they guard. The Sheldonian Theatre is rarely used for drama but regularly serves as a concert and lecture hall. Its main use is that for which it was built – university cere-monies. That is why you'll see the Chancellor's throne in a prominent position in the gilded auditorium. When Gilbert Sheldon, Archbishop of Canterbury and Chancellor of the university, commissioned the building in 1663, Wren, then Professor of Astronomy and a fellow of All Souls, based his design on a Roman theatre, hence the shape. The magnificent heads are thought to commemorate similar sculptures which decorated Roman boundary stones.

Carved head, Sheldonian Theatre

Look inside for the Chancellor's throne and for the magnificent ceiling painted by London artist Robert Streeter on 32 canvas panels showing the truth of arts and science triumphing over envy and ignorance. Now the Sheldonian plays host to the annual ceremonial Encaenia when honorary degrees are bestowed and speeches are made, following a procession through the city streets. It's worth climbing several flights of stairs to the cupola where – once you've recovered your breath – you'll be rewarded with a splendid view over the city.

Open: Mon–Sat 10.00–16.30 (closes 15.30 in winter)

Entry: under £5
Tel: 01865 277299
Website: www.sheldon.co.ac.uk
Disabled access: full to the theatre (best to ring in advance); none to cupola

Trinity College

Blades, Trinity College

Trinity College

Broad Street; map C3

Trinity has four splendid quadrangles and lovely gardens. You'll enjoy the wood carvings, believed to be the work of Grinling Gibbons, in the chapel. The wood used for the carvings is lime, pear, walnut and oak.

Open: daily; 10.00–12.00 and 14.00–16.00; (but Sat–Sun during termtime 14.00–16.00 only)
Entry: under £2
Tel: 01865 279900
Website: www.trinity.ox.ac.uk

Trinity College

University Church of St Mary the Virgin

University Church of St Mary the Virgin
High Street; map D3/D4

In the heart of the city, the 'official' university church has been the focal point of many nationally important events. The Oxford Martyrs, Anglican bishops Latimer, Ridley and Cranmer, were all brought to St Mary's for their trials; you can see a groove in a pillar in the north aisle where a platform was fixed for Archbishop Cranmer to stand and receive his sentence of death in 1556. John Wesley blotted his copybook here 200 years later when he preached against the laxity of the Church and the university. John Keble, professor of poetry, founded the so-called 'Oxford Movement' when he preached in St Mary's in 1833. John Newman, later to become a Cardinal after his conver-sion to Roman Catholicism, was vicar here from 1828–43. There are 127 steps up to the top of the tower – but the view is spectacular.

Open: daily; Jul–Aug: 9.00–19.00; Sep–Jun: 9.00–17.00
Entry: free to church but a visit to the tower costs under £2
Tel: 01865 279111
Website: www.university-church.ox.ac.uk
Disabled access: limited
Other facilities: gift shop

University Museum of Natural History
Parks Road; map C1

Megalosaurus footprints marking a trail across the expanse of green lawn in front of this wonderful museum gives you a clue that it's a fun place to visit. Outside the building looks imposing and municipal; walk in the door and you're in a graceful, light and airy space peopled –

University Museum of Natural History

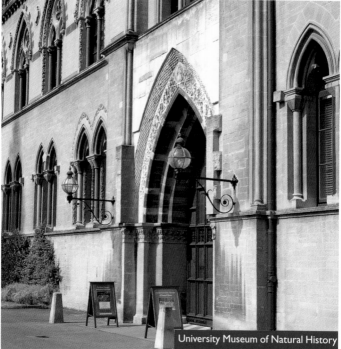

University Museum of Natural History
The 'Oxford' dodo

or animaled – by great dinosaur skeletons and cases of weird and wonderful
creatures. The building itself, soaring and
Gothic with decorative twiddles every-
where from wrought-iron foliage to
carved pillars, is an inspiring place to be;
the exhibits are the icing on the cake.

Here you'll find the painting of the
'Oxford' dodo and you can read how
this strange creature came to be closely
linked with Charles Dodgson (Lewis
Carroll) the creator of the book

TREAT YOURSELF
Make a date to visit Magdalen College in late April when the riverside meadows are covered, as far as the eye can see, in a haze of nodding pink and white snakeshead fritillaries.

Wadham College

Alice's Adventures in Wonderland. There are massive dinosaur skeletons – the largest collection of these incredible creatures outside London – and information and displays relating to hundreds of other creatures. There are minerals and rocks as well as shells and stones. In summer you can watch television pictures of the famous swifts nesting in the museum's tower via a live webcam. Best of all, it is completely free of charge.

Open: daily 12.00–17.00
Entry: free
Tel: 01865 272950
Website: www.oum.ox.ac.uk
Disabled access: full

Wadham College
Parks Road; map D2

This college was founded by a wealthy Somerset couple, neither of whom ever saw the completion of this lovely building. Nicholas Wadham died in 1609 before work could begin. The project was taken up with relish by his remarkable widow, Dorothy, who fought off other family claims on his will, found land and engaged Somerset builder/architect William Arnold (who also constructed Montacute House) to build to her instruction. Arnold, with a team of Somerset craftsmen, completed the whole operation within three years. Dorothy, working from Somerset, drew up the college statutes and appointed all the members, including the servants, but never visited the college herself. The hall and chapel are well proportioned and much of the building is original.

Open: daily; vacation: 10.30–11.45 and 13.00–16.15; term time: 13.00–16.15
Entry: free
Tel: 01865 277900
Website: www.wadham.ox.ac.uk

DOMINUS ILLUMINATIO MEA

WILLIAM MORRIS

William Morris – artist, poet and social critic – met fellow undergraduate Edward Burne-Jones at Exeter College in 1853. The pair changed their minds about careers in the Church and spent their lives in pursuit of excellent craft and design. A tapestry, designed by Burne-Jones and made by Morris, hangs in Exeter College chapel today.

BREATHING SPACE

Oxford's streets are wide and largely car-free (although you do have to look out for buses and bikes), so walking round the city is a pleasure. But if you feel the need to sit and relax for a while, there's plenty of green open space.

OXFORD-SPEAK

The Thames and its tributary the Cherwell flow through Oxford. But you'll hear the Thames referred to as 'Isis' (a shortening of its Latin name *Tamesis*), while you always pronounce the name of the other river as 'Charwul'.

University Parks

Botanic Garden

Botanic Garden; map F4

You will have to pay a small admission charge (around £2.50 for adults) in summer, but they're very happy for you to picnic or just sit and enjoy the peace and the remarkable plants in this, the oldest botanic garden in the country. The River Cherwell curls lazily round one side of the garden.

Christ Church Meadow; map D5–F6

Bring a picnic and comfortable shoes for a stroll around this remarkable open space, grazed by cattle and held in trust by Christ Church. You can get in via the War Memorial Garden (map C5) from St Aldates, from Merton Street (map D4) or Rose Lane (map E4)

Port Meadow

This ancient pastureland which has never been ploughed is reached from Walton Well Road at the top of Walton Street in north Oxford. The meadow is lovely in summer – but be warned that it does flood in winter and spring.

Port Meadow

Christ Church Meadow

which runs alongside the Botanic Garden. Which-ever way you enter, you're faced with paths that lead to the banks of the Thames and Cherwell or around the perimeter of the meadow. Gates to the meadow close at dusk.

Colleges

Most of the colleges are open to visitors in the afternoons only (see Sightseeing pages 32–55). Some, such as Christ Church, Trinity, Magdalen and Brasenose, offer pleas-ant places to sit awhile and enjoy a peaceful quad or a lovely garden. One of the prettiest college 'retreats' must be the strangely

named 'Deer Park' in Brasenose College. It's hard to imagine there being enough room for one deer, let alone a herd, in this delightful, sunny quadrangle, but it's a good place for a bit of quiet contemplation.

University Parks; map E1

This huge leafy green space in North Oxford is just the place for a stroll or a picnic. You can even walk to Mesopotamia – an area lying between two branches of the Cherwell.

SHOPPING

High-Street shops are better than average in Oxford, while independent retailers selling all manner of quality goods are to be found randomly throughout the city. This guide picks out some of the interesting shops both in the main retail areas and in more out-of-the-way streets. You'll find others as you make your way around the city.

Opening hours

Many shops open seven days a week, even during the winter. On Sundays opening hours are generally shorter than during the rest of the week.

David John (page 60)

Covered Market
map C3–C4

The biggest concentration of speciality food shops are in Oxford's wonderful Covered Market. Traditional butchers, fishmongers, greengrocers, cafés, speciality cheeses and a lot more are spread out side by side under one roof. You will find the entrances to the Covered Market either from The High (High Street) or through Market Street. Narrow lanes divide the stalls and shops and you'll probably have to walk up and down a few times to get your bearings.

Bread and cakes

Nash's Oxford Bakery sells all sorts of goodies including the sultana-stuffed Oxford lardy cake. If you stand outside The Cake Shop you'll be entertained and enticed as you watch the nimble-fingered icers and decorators working in the shop, making sugar flowers and wonderful confections to decorate the beautiful cakes on sale. And if you think triple-chocolate biscuits sound good, just visit Ben's Cookies.

The Cake Shop

Cheese

The Oxford Cheese Company is a national award winner. Their beautifully stocked stall is a magnet to all those who like traditionally produced

Oxford Cheese Company

farmhouse cheeses, including their own creamy and delicious Oxford Blue. You'll also find their famous Oxford Sauce among the 300 or so cheeses on display.

Chocology

£12.90

£19.90

tea and coffee company Cardew and Co. is here as well: they'll grind beans for you, supply you with all the gadgets for making good coffee, and sell decent cups to drink the resulting brew from.

Fish

Hayman's is the fishmongers to visit with lots of different kinds of fish to choose from.

Fruit and vegetables

If you can't find it at McCarthy Bros, you've imagined it – they have a huge range and supply many of the colleges with fruit and vegetables.

Meat

Carnivores are spoilt for choice with plenty of proper butchers' shops – from M. Feller, Son and Daughter, award-winning organic butchers, to David John, who makes 30 different varieties of sausage and sells wonderful old-fashioned delicacies such as gammon hocks.

R.R. Alden and Sons have

Chocolate

'There's nothing better than a good friend; except a good friend with chocolate', reads a sign in Chocology. Most of us would agree with that.

Delicatessens, tea and coffee

Palms Delicatessen celebrated its Golden Anniversary here in 2002 and you can see why it's so popular – it's got everything. Nearby is the tiny Italian deli, Fasta Pasta, stuffed to its colourful ceiling with tempting delicacies (try their olives); they do delicious sandwiches too. The long-established

Palms Delicatessen

been here since 1793 and is one of the country's oldest butchers. They specialize in rare-breed meats including local Oxford Down lamb and Oxford Sandyback pork.

Fashion

At the shop called Nothing they sell very good knitwear, bags, hats, jewellery and other bits and pieces, while Next to Nothing (no connection except its location) has good T-shirts and hippy-style skirts and trousers.

Two Foot Nothing (the joke goes on) is for young children. Crew Clothing stocks smart-casual yachty gear, while the Andean Craft Store has some distinctive sweaters and scarves. Shoe shops include the Oxford Boot Store, which has exciting Western-style boots – and hats. More hats – hundreds of them – are piled high in The Hat Box.

Books and other specialities

The Little Bookshop may

be small, but it's stuffed full of second-hand books – just the sort of place to find something you've been trying to get hold of for ages.

Other speciality shops include Brown's Leather Shop and The Oxford Engraver. The Garden and Jeminiare are both flower shops. You can nip into The Market Barber for a quick short back and sides or take worn-out shoes to The Market Cobbler to be repaired.

The Hat Box

The Garden

High-Street shops and department stores

The bulk of the usual High-Street names are found in Cornmarket Street (map C3–C4) and in the nearby Westgate and Clarendon shopping centres so these areas are always busy. Boswell's of Oxford is long-established on Broad Street (map C3), while Debenhams is just round the corner on Magdalen Street.

Books and music
Broad Street; map C3–D3

Start in the aptly named Broad Street where there is so much to see it's hard to know which way to turn. It is here you'll find Waterstone's and Blackwell's as well as Blackwell's Art and Posters and Blackwell's Music on the other side of the road. There's a snack bar, too, in the main store.

The High; map D4

You must look inside the illustrious University Press Bookshop.

Magdalen Street; map B3–C3

Here you'll find the popular American Borders

Bookstore, selling books and music, and food and drink in its café.

Turl Street; map C3

This ancient street is home to Unsworths Bookshop, selling second-hand books, especially history, literature and the humanities. The Classics Bookshop is here too.

St Aldates; map C4

Here you'll find The Oxford Music Shop which sells sheet music and a wide range of instruments from clarinets and flutes to guitars and drum kits.

St Michael's Street; map B3

If your book (or manuscript) needs to be bound, visit Maltby's, bookbinders.

Walton Street; map A1–A2

At the northern end of town in Walton Street is Thorntons of Oxford, selling second-hand volumes. Jericho Books is another Walton Street favourite.

Cakes and Patisserie
Woodstock Road; map B1

Oxford is full of shops selling all sorts of sweet

Maison Blanc

things to eat (particular favourites are the cinnamon and almond twists you see in many food shops), but if you're after a really special cake or tart, visit Maison Blanc to buy one of their little works of art. They do bread, good sweets and chocolate too.

Clothes for men
The High; map D4

Ede and Ravenscroft have been tailoring and making university and clerical clothes since as long ago as 1689. Shepherd and Woodward, too, are long-established outfitters.

Turl Street; map C3

Walters of Oxford is another traditional outfitters, while Ducker & Son has a shop window full of the best-polished shoes you'll see in the city.

Fashion

Broad Street; map C3–D3

Gaff, Isola and Diesel are all here.

Golden Cross Walk; map C4

This is where you'll discover Fresh with some beautiful clothes and accessories divided between two shops.

The High; map C4–E4

Here you'll find Narda Artwear, selling exotic, flowing silk coats, dresses and unusual hats. Agnes b and Whistles both sell designer outfits, while you should also look into Hobbs, Sahara and Jigsaw. Here, too, is Hampstead Bazaar with a wide range of smart casual clothes.

Little Clarendon Street; map B1

If you're in the Jericho area it's worth looking in at Annabel Harrison in Little Clarendon Street, just a step away. Hobbs have some lovely shoes and clothes and Lacy's offers a good range of fashion ideas. For something really different, try Uncle Sam's Vintage American Clothing which is just across the road.

St Michael's Street; map B3

DNA Clothes has an interesting selection, mainly for young and trendy shoppers.

Anne Day

Port Meadow

Ship Street; map C3
Retro clothes and accessories at Unicorn.

Walton Street; map A1
Anne Day in Walton Street in Oxford's trendy Jericho area is a small but well-stocked boutique and worth a visit. Port Meadow Designs in the same street sells clothing from around the world and jewellery too.

Homes and Gifts
The High; map C4–E4
Laurie Leigh sells beautiful and delicate antique glass (and keyboard instruments), while Pens Plus has a wonderful range of writing implements and boxes. Oxford Holographics will make you blink and stare as the objects for sale deceive your eyes. Sanders of Oxford have a shop full of rare prints and maps.

Uncle Sam's Vintage American Clothing

fresh

clothing

Fresh (page 64)

Central

Flowers from Daisies

selling paintings, ceramics
and elegant pieces made
by artists and craftsmen,
from stunning teapots to
bronze hares.

St Michael's Street;
map B3
Arcadia is full of gifts,
books, prints, cards and
souvenirs of Oxford.

Walton Street; map A1
The Corner Shop, just
opposite Little Clarendon
Street, is a place to
rummage through for a
woven kilim, antique
china, and bits and pieces
for the house and garden.
Look in Port Meadow
Designs too. And don't
miss Daisies, the florists.
They make up the most
beautiful hand-tied
bunches of flowers, taking
time to make sure they're
using the flowers you
would choose yourself.

Little Clarendon Street;
map B1
Try central for really stylish
designer furniture, glass
and gadgety things for the
kitchen, including all sorts
of coffee-makers and
toasters. They do lighting
and contemporary
tables and chairs as well.
Tumi is a shop with orna-
ments and clothes from
around the world. There's

always something colour-
ful to buy here.

Sylvester's sells a large
range of china, glass,
gifts, storage boxes and
baskets, while, a little
farther along the street,
Ottoman has some
unusual presents.

Get some good ideas at
Inspires, a small gallery

Woodstock Road;
map B1
Oriental Rug Gallery sells
particularly fine rugs and
carpets. You'll find Fired
Earth, the tile and home
furnishing shop, here too.

University Shops
You'll notice lots of shops
– some very old – selling
university colours and
souvenirs. They include
Fellows of Oxford and
The University of Oxford

Gift Shop in The High,
Flaggs The College Store
and The Varsity Shop in
Broad Street, and Walters
of Oxford in Turl Street.

**College and Museum
Gift Shops**
Many colleges and muse-
ums have excellent gift
shops (see pages 32–55).
You'll see the impressive
collection of college silver
as you enter the gift shop
for Christ Church in the
13th-century Chapter
House, where they sell an
excellent range of books,
cards and gifts. Books and
cards can also be bought at
the nearby Christ Church
Picture Gallery shop while
the Bodleian shop stocks
a very good selection of
Oxford-related gifts. More
reminders of your visit can
be found in the Ashmolean
Museum and the Bate
Collection shops.

Markets
Apart from the Covered
Market (see pages 59–61)
there is a street market
every Wednesday at
Gloucester Green (map
B3) while the popular
Farmers' Market, also at
Gloucester Green, is held
on the first Thursday of
every month.

Gloucester Green Market

Inspires

Artist: David Roade
Medium: Glass
Price: £255

Inspires (page 67)

EATING AND DRINKING

There's plenty of food for thought in Oxford but everyone needs more basic nourishment to keep body and soul together. Happily the city is well supplied with cafés, restaurants and pubs.

Cafés and café-bars serve every taste while the city has more than its fair share of very good restaurants. There are plenty of takeaway sandwich bars stuffed full of good things for people on the go. Those with a little more time will find that Oxford pubs are not only interesting and varied, but many do good food as well. Teatime is a peculiarly British ritual and you'll find some very grand teas – at a price. The list below is by no means exhaustive but it will give you some idea of what's on offer.

The Grand Café (page 72)

CAFES

Oxford has all the familiar names – Starbucks, Costa Coffee, Café Nero, Coffee Republic – and a lot more as well.

Brown's Café

Juice It

Covered Market; map C3–C4

For a really good choice, visit the Covered Market where you'll find Brown's serving the ultimate full

English breakfast and a good big mug of coffee or tea. If that's too hearty for you, try the vegetarian

Alpha Bar where you can eat in or take out salads, smoothies and dishes made with whole foods. Nearby is Juice It – you can't miss its bright orange decor – where they're big on wheatgrass and freshly squeezed juices. Café Morton, Brothers and Sofi de France all do coffee, sandwiches, panini and filled ciabatta. Upstairs is the well-loved Georgina's, brightly decorated, doing all-day breakfasts and the ultimate hot chocolate with whipped cream and marshmallow. Ricardo's Coffee Bar and Sandwich Shop and The Oxford Sandwich Company are handy for coffee and something to eat later.

Juice It

Golden Cross; map C4

Puccinos is part of a small chain but has an individual feel to it, with funky decor and decent Italian food.

The High; map E4

The Queen's Lane Coffee House is as long-established and comfortable as it appears. Across the way is the splendidly decorated Grand Café, which claims to be on the site of England's first coffee house (1650). They do good coffee and tea, delicious cakes and light lunches. If you want to send an email, go to Mices, an internet café.

Little Clarendon Street; map B1

If you like ice cream it's worth walking up here to George and Davis (known as G&D) Ice Cream Café. There is another, called George and Danvers, in St Aldates opposite Christ Church (map C5). The ice cream is home-made and very popular. Try the Oxford Blue.

St Michael's Street; map B3

Try the lumpy-bumpy cake at Meltz where you can also get a good lunch. Nearby is the more traditional Nosebag which has a daily selection of delicious salads.

Ship Street; map C3

The News Café has interesting food, good coffee and plenty of newspapers to read while you are drinking it.

Walton Street; map A1

The Jericho Café is deceptive in that there's a lot more space inside than you'd suspect and the food has a delicious Italian and Greek bias.

RESTAURANTS

It's worth looking towards north Oxford if you're after a special meal. The trendy Jericho area and the Banbury Road have lots of choice – but you'll also find plenty of places to eat in the centre of the city.

British
Cherwell Boathouse
50 Bardwell Road
Tie up your punt and enjoy the competent cooking and very good wine list at this renovated boathouse on the banks of the Cherwell.
Tel: 01865 552746

Parsonage Bar and Restaurant
1 Banbury Road; map B1
The surroundings are

Queen's Lane Coffee House

traditional but the food features surprises from around the world such as gingered chicken cakes and a fish green curry. There is plenty too for the less adventurous. The Parsonage is under the same ownership as Quod (see page 74) and Gees (see page 76).
Tel: 01865 310210

The Randolph Hotel
Beaumont Street;
map B2

Oxford's best-known hotel is always bustling with people meeting for drinks or coffee in the Morse Bar, enjoying cream teas, checking in for a luxury stay or dropping in for a meal in the restaurant or Oyster Bar. It's a treat-yourself place.
Tel: 0870 400 8200

Browns
5–11 Woodstock Road;
map B1

It's always comforting to know that you'll get the same friendly service and good brasserie-style food at whichever Browns you visit. Oxford's is delightfully smart and comfortable and the food is dependable.
Tel: 01865 511995

The Randolph Hotel

Fish
Fishers
36–37 St Clements Street
What's fresh in the market goes on the menu at this bright fish restaurant just off Magdalen Bridge. There is food for meat-eaters too, but the emphasis is on fish.
Tel: 01865 243003

French
Le Petit Blanc
71–72 Walton Street; map A1
There's a good value set menu here at lunchtime. Modern French cooking is matched by a wide choice of wines by the glass. Coffee and cakes are available all day.
Tel: 01865 510999

Browns (page 73)

TREAT YOURSELF
Try the excellent home-made ice cream at G&D's café in Little Clarendon Street or St Aldates. Take a child – or two or three children – with you and you have a good excuse for trying several of the delicious flavours.

Italian
Branca
111 Walton Street; map A1
Glass, steel, stone and wood combine to give a cool modern feel to this Italian restaurant. Risotto, pasta and pizza plus a special children's menu, well-chosen wines and desserts make eating here a pleasure.
Tel: 01865 556111

Quod Restaurant and Bar,
92–94 High Street; map D4
One of Oxford's newest and trendiest restaurants with modern, figurative paintings on the walls and a menu that encompasses chargrills, fish, risottos, pasta and pizza. Service is good and the surroundings pleasant.
Tel: 01865 202505

Quod Restaurant

Indian
The Bombay
82 Walton Street; map A1
In an area full of eateries
The Bombay doesn't
disappoint with reliable
cooking and pleasant
surroundings. You can bring
your own bottle of wine.
Tel: 01865 511188

Café Zouk
135 High Street; map C4

Expect good Moghal
cooking in this pleasant
first-floor restaurant.
Tel: 01865 251600

Chutneys
36 St Michael's Street;
map B3
This colourful restaurant
serves Indian and
Bangladeshi food in
pleasant surroundings.
Tel: 01865 724241

Mediterranean
Al Shami
25 Walton Crescent;
map A1
This Lebanese restaurant
is tucked-away in Walton
Crescent and is a favourite
with local people, who like
picking lots of different
dishes from the mix-and-
match menu and the good
choice of vegetarian food.
Tel: 01865 310066

Freud

Gees
61 Banbury Road
If you want a romantic dinner, book a table in this flower-filled Victorian conservatory and enjoy the whole experience. The modern European cooking, for example goat's cheese with aubergine and tomato, includes many fish dishes. Tel: 01865 553540

Thai and Far Eastern
Chiang Mai Kitchen
Kemp Hall Passage off The High; map C4
The food here is great – classic Thai cooking with a few Western twists. Try steamed scallops with chilli and garlic or the meaty pork dumplings. Tel: 01865 202233

The Mongolian Wok
67–69 George Street; map B3
You'll have fun here, selecting the raw ingredients for your meal and taking them up to be cooked by the man with the (giant) wok. And you can do it again and again. Eat early if you want to avoid the karaoke – or, on the other hand, eat late if you want to take part. Tel: 01865 792919

Freud
119 Walton Street; map A1
Apart from the weird sensation of eating in church (that's what the building was), you'll enjoy the Mediterranean cooking and the atmosphere here. Expect live music and friendly service. Tel: 01865 311171

PUBS

Oxford has many popular pubs; here are just a few of them.

The Bear

The Bear, Alfred Street; map C4

You must visit The Bear with its tiny bars, one of which has an extraordinary collection of snipped-off ties, all labelled and catalogued.

The Eagle and Child, St Giles; map B2

Called the Bird and Baby by some, this is a pub with history in St Giles. It is where those cronies, C.S. Lewis and J.R.R. Tolkien used to meet to discuss Middle Earth and Narnia. It is still a

good place to enjoy an hour or so; they do a great breakfast bap.

The Harcourt Arms, Cranham Terrace

A friendly local pub in the Jericho area.

Hobgoblin, St Aldates; map C5

The Hobgoblin is a small and interesting pub. It's open all day and serves reasonably priced food.

Kings Arms, Holywell Street; map D2

The Kings Arms has one big main bar and lots of side rooms to which you can retreat, read the newspapers, do the crossword (they supply the dictionary), play crib or video games. The food and beer are fine.

The Lamb and Flag, St Giles; map B2

This old, traditional pub is popular and often packed.

Old Tom, St Aldates; map C5

A no-frills pub. You can get a pavement table here if it's crowded inside.

Three Goats Heads, St Michael's Street; map B3

This unusually named pub has two bars, is nicely furnished and has a good choice of food with pleasant service.

Trout Inn, Lower Wolvercote; off the A34 Oxford bypass northbound

Out of town, this lovely, old riverside pub has views across to the abbey ruins.

Trout Inn

The Turf Tavern, Bath Place; map D3

The Turf Tavern is tucked between Holywell Street and New College Lane. There's a fine range of well-kept beer, the food is reasonable and the atmosphere terrific. In winter you can roast chestnuts and marshmallows on braziers. There's a good 'garden' for warmer days.

The Turl Bar, Turl Street; map C3

Tucked away in a courtyard off Turl Street, this is quiet, friendly and serves reasonable food.

White Horse, Broad Street; map D3

Sandwiched between two sections of Blackwell's bookshop, this pub is cosy, old and full of character.

TOP BOATS
The pub called The Head of the River at Folly Bridge (map C6) is named after the title awarded to the team winning the annual college 'Torpids' and 'Eights' knockout rowing races.

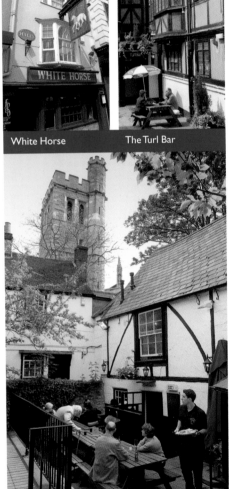

White Horse

The Turl Bar

The Turf Tavern

St Giles

AN EVENING OUT

As you would expect in a city full of enquiring minds and lively people, there's plenty to fill the hours before bedtime. Theatre, music, cinema, clubs, pubs galore and restaurants (see pages 72–76) are all within easy walking distance of the city centre.

A night at the theatre
The Oxford Playhouse in Beaumont Street (map B3) offers a wide range of productions from conventional drama, to dance, music and children's theatre. It also showcases new work. Rowan Atkinson and Dudley Moore both trod its boards before they became well known to stage and television audiences
Box office: 01865 305305

The New Theatre (previously the Apollo Theatre) in George Street (map B3) has a range of shows.
Box office: 0870 606 3500

Much smaller is the Burton Taylor Theatre, the studio space for the Playhouse. It's in Gloucester Green (map B3) and here you can see student productions, new plays and experimental drama as well.
Box office: 01865 305305

The productions at the Pegasus, Oxford's youth theatre, in Magdalen Road are often provocative
Box office: 01865 722851

There's a choice of entertainment at the Old Fire Station in George Street (map B3).
Box office: 01865 291170

Music, music, music
Music at Oxford presents a wonderful range of performances in the Sheldonian Theatre (map D3), Christ Church Cathedral (map D5), the Holywell Music Room (map D2/D3), the Jacqueline Du Pré music building at St Hilda's College (map F5) and Dorchester Abbey, just out of Oxford.
Tel: 0870 750 0659
Website: www.musicatoxford.com

Holywell Music Room

it's a converted church. An exotic touch of Morocco is offered at PoNaNa (tel: 01865 249171) in Magdalen Street (map B3).

Or a movie

There are Odeon cinemas (tel: 0870 505 0007) at Gloucester Green (map B3) and in Magdalen Street (map B3); The Phoenix Picture house (tel: 01865 512526) in Walton Street (map A1) has a comprehensive programme of classic cinema, art films, children's film and special events.

The renowned City of Oxford Orchestra has a full programme too.
Tel: 01865 744457
Website: www. cityofoxfordorchestra.co.uk

Walking with ghosts

The Ghost Tour starts at 20.00. Meet outside the Tourist Information Centre, Broad Street (map C3) at 19.45 on Friday and Saturday evenings from July to September – and at Hallowe'en.
Tel: 01865 726871

On the town

A city full of students is bound to have more than its share of nightclubs. Try Jongleurs (tel: 01865 722437) at Hythe Bridge Street (map A3) for a comedy evening, or on Tuesday nights only the Jericho Comedy Club Upstairs (tel: 01865 311775) at The Jericho in Walton Street (map A1). Then there's Freud (tel: 01865 311171) also in Walton Street where you can dance in the nave –

TOURS AND TRIPS

The best way to explore Oxford's nooks and crannies is on foot; walking tours led by knowledgeable and entertaining guides will help you do just that. There are bus tours, too, while the waterways can be explored by punt, skiff or a passenger trip on a steamer.

On foot

Tours of the city centre leave daily at 11.00 and 14.00 and are run on a 'first come first served basis'. Buy tickets (under £10) from the Tourist Information Centre (TIC) in Broad Street (map C3). There are extra tours on Saturday (also 11.00 and 14.00 from the TIC) which include admission to Christ Church.

Saturday is the day for the popular Inspector Morse tour. It's advisable to book in advance (under £10). It leaves at 13.30 and lasts two hours.
Tel: 01865 726871
Website:
tic@oxford.gov.uk

A board outside the University Church of St Mary the Virgin on The High (map D4) gives details of walking tours of the university.

By bus

Guide Friday do an open-topped bus tour with live commentary. Tickets are valid all day for the day you buy them, and you can hop on and off. Buy your ticket on the bus, at the TIC in Broad Street (map C3) or from the railway or bus station. Cost is under £10. Tours run daily throughout the year.
Tel: 01865 790522
Website: www.
guidefriday.com

Oxford Classic Tours also offer 'hop on and off' tours on open-top buses. Buy tickets from the kiosk in Bay 14 at Gloucester Green bus station (map B3) or directly from the driver. Cost is under £10.
Tel: 01865 790522
Website:
www.tappins.co.uk

On the water

Salters Steamers run daily trips between Oxford and Abingdon from mid-May to the end of September. They're based at Folly Bridge (map C6). If time is pressing you can take a shorter 40-minute return trip, or you can go-it-alone and, for £10 an hour,

Salters steamer

ROSAMUND THE FAIR

You can walk along the canal towpath to Wolvercote where, legend says, Fair Rosamund, the mistress of King Henry II, was murdered by a jealous Queen Eleanor and buried at nearby Godstow Nunnery.

hire a punt or skiff or, for £20–£40 an hour, an electric or diesel boat.
Tel: 01865 243421
Website: www. salterssteamers.co.uk

You can hire boats from the Cherwell Boathouse (01865 515978) as well or from C. Howard and Sons at Magdalen Bridge (map F4). Ring first or simply turn up.
Tel: 01865 202643
Website: www. oxfordpunting.com

Just a 30-minute drive away is Banbury where *Rosamund the Fair*, a narrow-boat restaurant, is now based. For just over £50 a head you get a gourmet four-course dinner (cooked to order on board) and can sit on deck between courses

to enjoy the 2.5-hour cruise. Book Saturday night dinner or Sunday lunch, or hire the whole boat for private parties.
Tel: 01295 278690 or

07831 616877
Website: www. rosamundthefair.co.uk

Punting on the river

WHAT'S ON

Many university customs have become annual events enjoyed by everyone in the city. Other festivals take place regularly throughout the year.

For more information on any of these events, please contact the Tourist Information Centre in Broad Street (map C3). Tel: 01865 726871 Website: www. visitoxford.org

February
Chinese New Year
Celebrations in Oxford Town Hall.
Tel: 01865 204188

Torpids
College rowing races on the Thames.

March
Torpids
College rowing races on the Thames.

International Women's Festival
Various venues. Live music, poetry, dance, theatre and exhibitions.
Tel: 01865 553755

April
Sunday Times Oxford Literary Festival
Oxford Union, St Michael's Street.
Tel: 01865 514149

May
May Morning
Magdalen College Choir sings from the top of Magdalen Tower at 6.00 on 1 May. Celebrations on riverbanks and Morris dancing in Radcliffe Square and Broad Street.

Annual Balloon Fiesta
Held in Cutteslowe Park.
Tel: 01865 467259

Oxford Fun Run
Starts at University Parks, Parks Road.
Tel: 01993 881368

Lord Mayor's Parade
On the late May Bank Holiday from the city centre to end at South Parks, where there is children's entertainment and arena events.

Eights Week
Four days of inter-collegiate rowing races on the Thames.

Torpids

Beating the Bounds

Traditional ceremony on Ascension Day where townspeople visit ancient town boundaries (including one in the middle of Marks and Spencer) after a service at 9.00 at the Church of St Michael at the North Gate.

June

East Oxford Carnival

A colourful multi-cultural celebration processing from Cowley Road to Manzil Way, with live bands and entertainment.
Tel: 01865 467259

Encaenia

University ceremony held in the Sheldonian Theatre where, after a procession of university dignitaries, honorary degrees are conferred.

Oxford Canal Festival

A celebration of life and customs on the waterway. Held by the waterside at Aristotle Road recreation ground.
Tel: 01865 467259

July

Festival of Sport

A two-day celebration of football, basketball, hockey, volleyball and other sports

St Giles' Fair

for all the family held in Cutteslowe Park.
Tel: 01865 467259

August

Jazz in the Park

One-day family music event at South Parks.
Tel: 01865 467259

Oxford City Royal Regatta

Competitors from all over the country take part in races along the Thames from Folly Bridge to Long Bridges over two days.
Tel: 07785 283291

September

St Giles' Fair

Two-day street funfair dating back to 1625. Fairground rides, stalls in St Giles, Magdalen Street, Beaumont Street, Woodstock Road and Banbury Road.

December

Lord Mayor's Christmas Carols

Held in the Town Hall.

Morris Dancing

At Headington Quarry on Boxing Day.

Encaenia

OXFORD FOR KIDS

The city that provided the inspiration for Philip Pullman's Jordan College and the film location for J.K. Rowling's Hogwarts School dining hall has everything going for it as far as youngsters are concerned. There's plenty of outdoor fun to be had on the river and in the parks, while imaginative museums offer much to keep children happily occupied.

Magical moments

All kids will recognize the great dining hall at Christ Church as the setting for the hall at Hogwarts, where Harry Potter learns his wizard profession. They'll also be keen on the link between Exeter College and Lyra Belacqua, the girl in Phillip Pullman's *Northern Lights* who takes on evil and wins. Younger children will enjoy the Alice in Wonderland connection (see page 19). After visiting Christ Church you can go to the nearby Alice's Shop and café.

Dinosaurs and all that

Oxford youngsters are amazingly lucky to have free use of the University Museum of Natural History (see page 52) – young visitors can't fail to enjoy the cleverly exhibited dinosaurs and other animals in this very welcoming building. It's just a step through to the Pitt Rivers Museum (see page 46), which has so many exhibits that you'll have to be selective. Many kids will love the shrunken heads and look out for the regular 'Pitt Stops' – free family activities. Nearer the city centre in Beaumont Street is the Ashmolean Museum (see page 34) with a very good programme of children's events.

A trip through time

The Oxford Story (see page 46) in Broad Street is a 45-minute 'dark' ride through centuries of Oxford history – sights, sounds, smells and all.

Ask me another

If you've always wanted to know how to lift an elephant, visit the Old Fire Station in George Street, where the hands-on science workshop, Curioxity, will tell you. Children, and adults too, will have a lot of fun here, playing with strange machines and following the Curioxitrail around the city.

Light refreshment

Delicious home-made ice cream, including the curiously coloured Oxford Blue, will be devoured and enjoyed at G&D's ice-cream cafés. There's one in Little Clarendon Street (map B1) and another on St Aldates (map C5).

Alice's Shop

Christ Church dining hall

OUT OF TOWN

If you want to explore the rolling countryside around Oxford there are plenty of interesting focal points for a trip out of town. Here are a few suggestions.

Blenheim Palace, Woodstock

8 miles north-west of Oxford on the A44 towards Evesham

A grateful Queen Anne decided to reward John Churchill, the 1st Duke of Marlborough, with the gift of the Manor of Woodstock and a house to be called 'Blenheim' after his famous victory in battle there. Work started on the house in 1712 but was halted when the poor Duke fell out of favour and the royal bounty dried up.

However Blenheim was eventually built and is the extravagant creation of architects John Vanbrugh and Nicholas Hawksmoor with a park landscaped by 'Capability' Brown. It is the birthplace of Winston Churchill and there is a permanent exhibition devoted to the great man. The Marlborough Maze is one of the biggest in the world and contains a model street, a putting green and a giant chess set. You should allow the best part of a day to see the house, the maze, the gardens, butterfly house and park.

Tel: 01993 811091

Website: www. blenheimpalace.com

Blenheim Palace

Cotswold Wildlife Park

Cotswold Wildlife Park, Burford
18 miles west of Oxford on the A40 and A361
Children and adults alike will enjoy this most interesting mix of animals and exotic plants. The 65 hectares (160 acres) of parkland are not only home to 200 species of animals but are also imaginatively planted so that gardeners will be as excited as wildlife enthusiasts. There's plenty to do and see (insect house, children's farmyard, reptile house, walled garden, tropical house) and the whole place feels like a haven.
Tel: 01993 823006
Website: www.cotswoldwildlifepark.co.uk

White Horse Hill, near Uffington
20 miles south-west of Oxford via A34, A417 and B4507
The amazing, sinuous white horse carved in the chalk of the high hills has been there for 3,000 years, say Oxford University archaeologists. You can see it best from a distance and then park nearby to follow the ancient Ridgeway track on foot westwards to Wayland's Smithy, a 5,000-year-old burial chamber.

Didcot Railway Centre, Didcot
10 miles south of Oxford, signposted from A34
The great days of steam are recreated here with a huge collection of Great Western Railway steam engines, wagons, coaches and buildings. Thomas the Tank Engine pays frequent visits. Enjoy the rides and the steamdays.
Tel: 01253 8172000
Website: www.didcotrailwaycentre.org.uk

White Horse Hill

WHERE TO STAY

From grand and traditional to cosy farmhouse bed and breakfast, there is accommodation for all tastes and pockets in and around Oxford. The Tourist Information Centre (see page 94) has a complete list of hotels, guest houses, bed and breakfasts, pubs, self-catering cottages, and caravan and camp sites. The list below will give you some idea of the range on offer. Check facilities and prices before booking.

Prices
The £ symbols are an approximate guide for comparing the prices charged, which range from about £25 to over £100 per person per night.

The Randolph Hotel
Beaumont Street; map B2
The Randolph has 114 rooms and is one of Oxford's best-loved hotels. Meet for a drink in the Inspector Morse bar before you have dinner in the restaurant or enjoy lunch in the elegant Oyster Bar.
Tel: 0870 400 8200
Website: www.macdonald-hotels.com
£££

Old Parsonage Hotel
1 Banbury Road; map B1
This lovely historic house has 30 beautifully furnished bedrooms and a very good restaurant. There's a large garden to wander in and a roof garden too. It belongs to a small group of hotels and restaurants in the area.
Tel: 01865 310210
Website: www.oxford-hotels-restaurants.co.uk
£££

Bath Place Hotel
4 and 5 Bath Place; map D3
This charming, small hotel was once a cluster of 17th-century cottages. It is tucked away between two colleges in the heart of Oxford. There are 13 rooms in all, each with its own bathroom.
Tel: 01865 791812
Website: www.bathplace.co.uk
£££

College Guest House
103–105 Woodstock Road; map B1
Just a few minutes walk from the city centre in leafy Woodstock Road, this nicely furnished guest house has 18 rooms and is a friendly place to stay.
Tel: 01865 552579
Website: www.collegeguesthouse.oxfordpages.co.uk
££

Marlborough House Hotel
321 Woodstock Road
They do bed and break-

The Randolph Hotel (page 91)

fast here but all 14 rooms also have a kitchenette if you want to self-cater.
Tel: 01865 311321
Website: www. oxfordcity.co.uk/hotels/ marlborough
££

The Falcon Private Hotel
88/90 Abingdon Road; map C6
This friendly, small hotel just outside the city centre has 12 rooms, all with en suite facilities.
Tel: 01865 511122
Website: www.oxfordcity. co.uk/hotels/falcon
££

Manor Farmhouse
Manor Road, Bladon
Bed and breakfast is offered in this old farm-house which has one twin and one double bedroom for guests. Bladon is a village 6 miles north-west of the city.
Tel: 01993 812168
££

The Old House
Akeman Street, Combe
There are just two beauti-fully furnished bedrooms at this elegant stone house offering bed and breakfast in a village about 10 miles north-west of Oxford.

Tel: 01993 898216
££

Oxford Youth Hostel
2A Botley Road
This purpose-built guest accommodation, just 5 minutes walk from the city centre, offers 184 beds in clean and

comfortable budget rooms. There's full access for disabled guests. You can join the YHA when you arrive and, although it's a youth hostel, there is no age limit!
Tel: 01865 727275
Website: www.yha.org.uk
£

Bath Place Hotel (page 91)

USEFUL INFORMATION

TOURIST INFORMATION

Tourist Information Centre (TIC) 15–16 Broad Street, Oxford OX1 3AS; (map C3)

Extensive services include accommodation booking; travels, attractions and events information; a bureau de change; maps and guides.

Open: daily; Mon–Sat 9.30–17.00; Sun and public holidays 10.00–13.00 and 13.30–15.30 during the summer. Closed from 25 Dec to 1 Jan

Tel: 01865 726871

Website: www. visitoxford.org

What's On

For what is happening on any particular day look in *This Month in Oxford* (free from newsagents) or in the daily newspaper, *Oxford Mail.*

Guided walks

Official guided walking tours leave the Tourist Information Centre daily at 11.00 and 14.00; tel: 01865 726871.

Inspector Morse walk; tel: 01865 726871.

The Ghost Walk, Jul–Sep and on 31 Oct; tel: 01865 726871.

TRAVEL

Airport

The nearest airport is Birmingham.

Tel: 0121 767 5511

Bus information

The bus and coach station is at Gloucester Green; map B3.

Two coach companies make regular trips to and from London (approx 100 mins journey time): Oxford Stagecoach tel: 01865 772250.

Citylink tel: 01865 785400.

National Express run services in Oxfordshire tel: 08705 808080.

Rail information

Oxford railway station is at the far end of Park End Street (map A3) and is a 10-minute walk west of the city centre.

Thames Trains run frequent services to London Paddington, while Virgin Trains offer services via Oxford. For all timetable and fare information phone the National Rail Enquiry Service on 08457 484950.

Taxis

There are taxi ranks at the railway station, at Gloucester Green coach station and at St Giles (map B2) in the centre of the city.

Bike Hire

Bike Zone, Market Street; map C3

Tel: 01865 728877

Shopmobility

Free use of powered wheelchairs or scooters for those with limited mobility. Oxford Shopmobility is located on Level 1a of Westgate Shopping Centre Car Park (map B5). Operates Mon–Fri 9.30–16.00. Book on 01865 248737.

PARK AND RIDE
map: see page 100

Parking in the city centre is expensive and restricted. Oxford City Council encourage motorists to use the five park-and-ride services instead. They offer frequent non-stop buses to central Oxford and are cheap and easy to use.

Redbridge Park and Ride

To the south-west of Oxford and signposted from the A34. Operates daily; Mon–Sat 5.30–23.30, buses leave every 6 mins (every 30 mins early morning and evening); Sun 8.45–19.03, buses leave every 20 mins until 10.45, then every 15 mins.

Pear Tree Park and Ride

To the north-east of Oxford, signposted from A34 and A4260. Operates daily; Mon–Sat 5.30–23.28, buses leave every 6 mins (every 30 mins early morning and evening); Sun 8.40–18.58, buses leave every 20 mins until 11.00, then every 15 mins.

Water Eaton Park and Ride

To the north-east of the city at Kidlington. Operates Mon–Sat 7.00–19.00; closed on Sunday. Buses run Mon–Sat 7.00–19.08.

Thornhill Park and Ride

On the east of Oxford. Operates daily; Mon–Sat 5.30–23.30, buses leaves every 10–11 mins (every 30 mins early morning and evening); Sun 8.20–21.30, buses leave every 30 mins until 9.50, every 20 mins afterwards.

Seacourt Park and Ride

On the west of Oxford. Operates daily; Mon–Sat 7.00–19.00, buses leave every 10 mins (every 30 mins early morning and evening); Sun 8.20–21.34, buses leave every 20 mins during the day, every 30 mins early morning and evening.

BANKS
Cash dispensers
Barclays, Cornmarket Street; map C4
HSBC, Cornmarket Street; map C4
Lloyds TSB, High Street; map C4
Royal Bank of Scotland, St Giles; map B2

MAIN POST OFFICE
St Aldates; map C4

ICE RINK
Oxford Ice Rink, Oxpens Road; map A5
Tel: 01865 248076

EMERGENCIES
Fire, ambulance or police
Tel: 999

Oxford Police Station
St Aldates; map C6
Tel: 01865 266000

John Radcliffe Hospital
Headington Way (includes accident and emergency department)
Tel: 01865 741166

Extended-hours pharmacy
Ten o'Clock Pharmacy, 59 Woodstock Road; (map B1); opens daily 9.00–22.00
Tel: 01865 515226

24-hour petrol station
Oxpens Service Station (Esso), Oxpens Road; map A5
Tel: 01865 721397

24-hour breakdown
Isis Rescue, Cowley, Oxford
Tel: 01865 434343

INDEX

CITY-BREAK GUIDES

These full-colour guides come with stunning new photography capturing the special essence of some of Britain's loveliest cities. Each is divided into easy-reference sections where you will find something for everyone – from walk maps to fabulous shopping, from sightseeing highlights to keeping the kids entertained, from recommended restaurants to tours and trips ... and much, much more.

BATH

Stylish and sophisticated – just two adjectives that sum up the delightful Roman city of Bath, which saw a resurgence of popularity in Georgian times and in the 21st century is once again a vibrant and exciting place to be.

CAMBRIDGE

Historic architecture mingles with hi-tech revolution in the university city of Cambridge, where stunning skylines over surrounding fenland meet the style and sophistication of modern city living.

CHESTER

Savour the historic delights of the Roman walls and charming black-and-white architecture, blending seamlessly with the contemporary shopping experience that make Chester such an exhilarating city.

OXFORD

City and university life intertwine in Oxford, with its museums, bookstores and all manner of sophisticated entertainment to entice visitors to its hidden alleyways, splendid quadrangles and skyline of dreaming spires.

STRATFORD

Universally appealing, the picturesque streets of Stratford draw visitors back time and again to explore Shakespeare's birthplace, but also to relish the theatres and stylish riverside town that exists today.

YORK

A warm northern welcome and modern-day world-class shops and restaurants await you in York, along with its ancient city walls, Viking connections and magnificent medieval Minster rising above the rooftops.

Jarrold Publishing, Healey House, Dene Road, Andover, Hampshire, SP10 2AA, UK

Sales: 01264 409206
Enquiries: 01264 409200
Fax: 01264 334110
e-mail: heritagesales@jarrold-publishing.co.uk
website: www.britguides.com

MAIN ROUTES IN AND OUT OF OXFORD

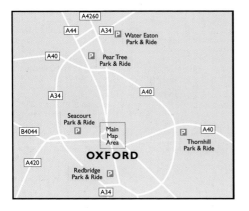

Park and ride services leave regularly for central Oxford from:

Pear Tree Park and Ride
Signposted from the A34 and A4260

Water Eaton Park and Ride
Signposted from the A4260

Thornhill Park and Ride
Junction 8 on the M40, signposted from the A40

Redbridge Park and Ride
Signposted from the A34

Seacourt Park and Ride
Signposted from the A420 and B4044

See page 95 for further details